ARCHITECTURE FC
THE COMMONS

Architecture for the Commons dives into an analysis of how the tectonics of a building is fundamentally linked to the economic organizations that allow them to exist. By tracing the origins and promises of current technological practices in design, the book provides an alternative path, one that reconsiders the means of achieving complexity through combinatorial strategies. This move requires reconsidering serial production with crowdsourcing and user content in mind. The ideas presented will be explored through the design research developed within Plethora Project, a design practice that explores the use of video game interfaces as a mechanism for participation and user design.

The research work presented throughout the book seeks to align with a larger project that is currently taking place in many different fields: The Construction of the Commons. By developing both the ideological and physical infrastructure, the project of the Commons has become an antidote to current economic practices that perpetuate inequality. The mechanisms of the production and governance of the Commons are discussed, inviting the reader to get involved and participate in the discussion. The current political and economic landscape calls for a reformulation of our current economic practices and alternative value systems that challenge the current market monopolies.

This book will be of great interest not only to architects and designers studying the impact of digital technologies in the field of design but also to researchers studying novel techniques for social participation and cooperating of communities through digital networks. The book connects principles of architecture, economics and social sciences to provide alternatives to the current production trends.

Jose Sanchez is an Architect, Game Designer and Theorist based in Detroit, Michigan. He is the director of the Plethora Project (www.plethora-project.com), a research studio investing in the future of the propagation of architectural design knowledge. He is the creator of the award-winning video game *Block'hood*, a city simulator exploring notions of ecology, entropy, and interdependence, and the creator of *Common'hood*, a video game social platform that enables the authoring of architectural design within Creative Commons. He is also the co-creator of Bloom, a crowd sourced interactive installation which was the winner of the Wonder Series hosted by the City of London for the 2012 Olympics.

He has taught in renowned institutions in the United States and in Europe, including the Architectural Association in London, The Bartlett School of Architecture at University College London, at the University of Southern California, and is currently at the University of Michigan where he is an Associate Professor in the School of Architecture. His research "Gamescapes" explores generative interfaces in the form of video games, speculating on modes of intelligence augmentation, combinatorics and open systems as design mediums.

ARCHITECTURE FOR THE COMMONS

Participatory Systems in the Age of Platforms

Jose Sanchez

Routledge
Taylor & Francis Group

LONDON AND NEW YORK

First published 2021
by Routledge
2 Park Square, Milton Park, Abingdon, Oxon OX14 4RN

and by Routledge
52 Vanderbilt Avenue, New York, NY 10017

Routledge is an imprint of the Taylor & Francis Group, an informa business

© 2021 Jose Sanchez

British Library Cataloguing-in-Publication Data
A catalogue record for this book is available from the British Library

Library of Congress Cataloging-in-Publication Data
Names: Sanchez, Jose, 1980- author.
Title: Architecture for the commons / Jose Sanchez.
Description: New York : Routledge, 2020. | Includes bibliographical
    references and index.
Identifiers: LCCN 2019057773 (print) | LCCN 2019057774 (ebook) |
    ISBN 9781138362352 (hardback) | ISBN 9781138362369 (paperback) |
    ISBN 9780429432118 (ebook)
Subjects: LCSH: Architectural design—Philosophy. |
    Information commons.
Classification: LCC NA2500 .S145 2020 (print) | LCC NA2500 (ebook) |
    DDC 729/.01—dc23
LC record available at https://lccn.loc.gov/2019057773
LC ebook record available at https://lccn.loc.gov/2019057774

ISBN: 978-1-138-36235-2 (hbk)
ISBN: 978-1-138-36236-9 (pbk)
ISBN: 978-0-429-43211-8 (ebk)

Typeset in Bembo
by Apex CoVantage, LLC

To Catherine

CONTENTS

FIGURES

ACKNOWLEDGMENTS

This book has been the result of many years of conversations and discussions between a generation of architects that have found the need to expand the framing of technology in architecture. The notion of Discrete Architecture, as discussed in this volume, has been a collective project that remains diverse in its motivations and expectations. At it's core, is an interest to question and actively redefine the socio-political role of the tools we architects use. The group that has framed Discrete Architecture has been composed of peers such as Gilles Retsin, Daniel Koehler, Rasa Navasaityte, Phillippe Morel, Emmanuelle Chiappone-Piriou, Mollie Claypool, Ryan Manning and Manuel Jimenez Garcia. Beyond the advocacy for a discrete methodology, it has been central for this project to engage in public forums where I would like to acknowledge the earnest feedback of Mario Carpo, Frederic Migayrou, Casey Rehm, Marrikka Trotter, Damjan Jovanovic, Viola Ago, Ramon Weber, Manja van de Worp, Igor Pantic and Soomeen Hahm, who have contributed to the definition of what we have denominated Discrete Design.

Architecture for the Commons is a book that departs from the collective project of the discrete agenda and aims to frame the larger socioeconomical imperatives present in our current information society. The social awareness that drives this project was founded in my education at the Universidad in Chile and has been a motivation through my years in academia in London and Los Angeles. It has been at the Architectural Association in London, within the Design Research Laboratory, where a critical approach toward parametric design has initially developed, in particular by a generation that studied under Patrik Schumacher, who has always been a generous respondent to the criticism presented throughout symposiums and conversations.

This book would not be possible without a strong community of architects, theorists and technologists who have engaged with fragments of this book throughout many years, in particular the Acadia community where I would like to acknowledge the support provided in conversations by Kathy Velikov, Jason Kelly-Johnson, Adam Marcus, Andrew Kudless, Andrew Payne, Kory Beig, Dana Cupkova, Lauren Vasey, Branko Kolarevic, Behnaz Farahi, Aldo Sollazzo and Ersela Kripa.

The direction taken in this volume since early versions of the manuscript has received generous support and feedback from a large group of people who helped me find the angle to discuss my concerns regarding technology, social issues and the economy. I would like to thank the feedback from Peggy Deamer, Marcelyn Gow, Skylar Tibbits, Gilles Retsin, Mollie Claypool and Daniel Köhler, who provided critical feedback at different points of the development of the manuscript.

There is also an important number of institutions that have facilitated the discussions of the content of this volume with faculty and students. These include the Bartlett School of Architecture, with the support of Frederic Migayrou, Bob Sheil, Marcos Cruz, Mario Carpo and Roberto Botazzi; The Architectural Association, with the support of Alicia Nahmad; The Institute for Advanced Architecture of Catalonia, with the support of Areti Markopoulou and Tomaz Diez; California College of Arts, with the support of Adam Marcus, Nataly Gattegno and Jason Kelly-Johnson; Berkeley School of Architecture with the support of Ronald Rael; Texas A&M School of Architecture with the support of Gabriel Esquivel; and the Massachusetts Institute of Technology with the support of Paloma Gonzales Rojas.

For the last six years, it has been my own institution, The School of Architecture at the University of Southern California, that has supported me and encouraged me to continue with and complete this contribution. I am thankful to all the faculty but in particular to those who made time out of their busy schedules to discuss with me early versions of the manuscript and my ideas, including Vittoria di Palma, Diane Ghirardo, Jim Steele, Alvin Huang, Amy Murphy, Kim Coleman, Chuck Lagreco, Victor Regnier, Doris Sung and Alex Robinson.

Alongside my colleagues, there have been many students and alumni that have engaged with my ideas and contributed to the formulations presented in this book. Out of many students over the last eight years of academia, I would like to thank for their contributions Joshua Dawson, Gentaro Makinoda, Jingbo Yan, Decheng Zeng, Lienny Ruiz, George Tsakiridis, Efthymia Kotsani and Mingfeng Xia.

I would also like to acknowledge the ideas of influential people throughout my career who have inspired and challenged the ideas presented in this book. These include Casey Reas, Peggy Deamer, Karsten Schmidt, Will Wright and Neil Gershenfeld.

The time and effort to complete this book wouldn't have been possible without the support of a design team that has engaged and developed the ideas of my design studio, the Plethora Project. I would like to profoundly thank the support of Satrio Dewantono, Brendan Ho, Kellan Cartledge, Jiachen Wei and in particular of Ban Sheni, who has helped me directly in the structuring of this publication. I would also like to thank colleagues in Chile who contributed to projects and discussions connected to ideas in this book; these include Camilo Guerrero, Matias Honorato, Diego Pinochet and Felipe Veliz.

I would also like to acknowledge the fantastic work of Ryan Tyler Martinez who designed the cover of this book.

I would like to express my profound gratitude to my family in Chile for all of their support and especially their sacrifices due to the physical distance between us: my parents Jose Victor Sanchez and Yolanda Recio, and my siblings Graciela Sanchez, César Sanchez, Belen Sanchez and Juan Pablo Sanchez. Finally, this publication would not have come to fruition without my partner, Catherine Griffiths, who has discussed with me every single idea presented here. This publication would not have been possible without her scrutiny and encouragement. I'm eternally thankful.

INTRODUCTION

A call for a post-2008 architecture

We have always been parametric

At the end of the 20th century, recent innovations in architecture were proposing a fundamental shift in the way that we understand and construct buildings. Technological innovations in software, material science, digital fabrication and automation offered a vision of infinite variability and customization. This vision engaged with human perception, defining an affective architecture tailored as an immersive environment.[1] This ever-changing "new" architecture, where every design is a "one-off," has become a core part of the current practice of a younger generation of architects. It has been validated by narratives around technology: the promise that digital fabrication, operated by CNC technology, could produce bespoke forms at an equivalent cost to a mass-produced product provided the perfect argument for adopting an ever-changing architecture.[2] Mass-produced products had defined other industries for many years, but CNC technology was promising to offer a liberating alternative, one in which design would flourish and would be constantly in demand, as clients will always be in search of a fresh new design proposal.

The implications of continuously supporting a paradigm of "one-off" architecture, which has to reinvent itself in every building, has ramifications that span from the tectonic composition of the built environment to the business models and commission allocations in practice. It has also deeply influenced the education culture of the field, preparing students to engage with a highly competitive marketplace where it is a commonplace to work for free or engage in underpaid or exploitative practices due to the unremunerated format of design proposals.[3] This is the result of a high volume of design labor that goes to waste by speculative business practices of clients or architectural competition entries that have little to no chance of success.

Within this context, the rise of the parametric paradigm can be understood as a response to the core inefficiencies in the field. Understanding the design variations that a proposal will need throughout its development, the parametric paradigm has offered a technical workflow where an architect does not design one building but rather a multiplicity of virtual buildings, all ruled by variable data. Whether there are changes in the budget, regulation or simply a change of heart of a client, parametric software has allowed architects to design hundreds of possible designs by defining buildings not as objects but rather by associations and proportions between elements, maintaining an overall consistency throughout a network. Out of this virtual multiplicity, thousands of designs can be eliminated without incurring much of a loss, as it is only one of those models that moves forward to be realized.

The multiplicity of virtual buildings allowed by the parametric methodology can be seen as a triumph of capitalist productivity, where the labor of one designer is exponentially multiplied, allowing the possibility of defining a whole city, one in which every single building can be singular. This technical and conceptual project was explored in the ideas of "parametric urbanism"[4] by Patrik Schumacher within Zaha Hadid Architects, at the Architectural Association and at the University of Innsbruck. The arguably utopian vision of parametric urbanism proposed a unified algorithmic style that could rule the variation of every building and detail of a city or district, adapting buildings to local site conditions. The utopianism behind this proposition was not only in the visual or stylistic coherence between buildings as argued by Schumacher[5] but also in the potential triumph of the ability to scale the labor and vision of a single designer to operate over a large territory.

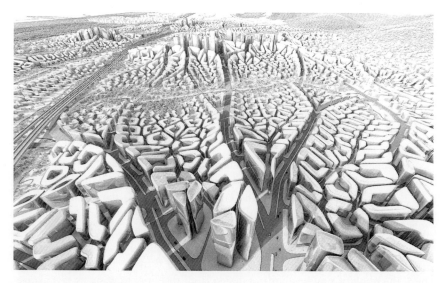

FIGURE I.1 Parametric Urbanism by Research led by Patrik Schumacher. Design proposal led by Ursula Frick and Thomas Grabner at the University of Innsbruck, Austria.

In reality, the parametric model, while it has allowed for mass customization and the differentiation of hundreds or even thousands of different building parts, has failed to scale the domain of influence of a single designer. The virtual multiplicity existing within a parametric definition generates a pool of competing proposals out of which only one will be taken forward for execution. The multiplicity of the virtual equates to a singular actual.

Clients have come to expect the possibility of exploring the domain of the design potential, expecting to see proposals that address a brief in radically different ways. After all, the substantial amount of capital that is required to develop architecture has made common sense for both the private and public sectors to require a large amount of design proposals to be available before taking a final decision about what will become a permanent part of the built environment. The parametric model is ill-equipped to perform such a task, as a parametric definition has demonstrated to be better suited to offer the variation of a proposal and not fundamentally different proposals. Parametric differentiation is a change in degree, not in kind.

Nevertheless, the public and the private sector for years have collaborated with architects to take part of a form of procurement that allows for a quick production of a multiplicity of radically different proposals, each of them with a careful consideration of the building constraints. This is known as the architectural competition. This technique can be considered the ultimate parametric modeling methodology, as it is able to produce a large virtual multiplicity, with substantial design variation practically for free for the client, at great expense from participants. The resulting catalog of proposals is often tossed aside as the unsuccessful attempts of an equation that has been designed to define a singular winner.

Architectural competitions follow all the principles of a parametric design methodology, offering cheap design variations exploring the possibility space of a building. The problem arises when one understands that parametric design discards 99% of digitally created possible buildings, design proposals that are generated algorithmically as the result of the declaration of design decisions as variables. On the other hand, an architectural competition discards the 99% of designs generated by the unremunerated labor of architects that have been orchestrated as a competing pool to arrive at a suitable solution. Architecture competitions are nothing new to the field, as they are a long-standing practice deeply ingrained in architectural culture. Architectural competitions, therefore, remind us that we have always been parametric, as our freely offered labor validates practices of unremunerated speculative work.

Architectural competitions have validated Patrik Schumacher's claim that the parametric agenda is an epochal style.[6] However, they have not done so through Schumacher's argument of an emergent aesthetic of articulation between free market agents but rather by a global acceptance of a procurement technique that is able to extract free value out of thousands of practicing architects through their aspirations to contribute to the advancement of the discipline and to obtain a remunerated commission. The epoch that parametric design defines is that of neoliberal economics, operating under a "winner takes all" ideology and a "trickle-down" form of propagation of knowledge, where innovation developed for avant-garde projects is gradually supposed to reach societal adoption. This has not occurred. On the contrary, a pursuit for the always new "one-off" building leaves little room for cultural adoption. The winner-takes-all model has created large asymmetries of power, capital and wealth.

The polarization of architecture

The pursuit of architectural innovation through commercial means depends on large accumulations of capital. Architects for centuries have come to cherish the possibility of finding a client that could operate as a benefactor for the development of their architectural vision. An iconic example can be studied in the relationship that Frank Gehry established with Peter Lewis and the development of the Lewis Residence. As noted by Paul Goldberg, the reputation of Gehry allowed him to gather rich and adventurous clients, where Peter Lewis, who had earned billions in the insurance business, would spend six years and more than $6 million in fees having Gehry design multiple versions of an $82 million house that Lewis would ultimately choose not to build.[7] Gehry later acknowledged that the support received by Lewis equated to his receiving a MacArthur "Genius Grant," money that would allow Gehry to develop his most advanced ideas with no strings attached.[8]

It is fair to say that there are not enough clients like Peter Lewis and that it is unrealistic to cultivate such design expectations in architectural education. Nevertheless, a disproportionate amount of architectural research and education is dedicated to commissions that could only be supported by such an improbable client.

The field has become aware of this disproportionate interest for artistic exercise and has articulated a backlash in recent years. Architecture has attempted to rediscover an ethical compass by emphasizing humanitarian and low-income projects. The 2016 Venice Architecture Biennial, curated by Chilean architect Alejandro Aravena, emphasized architects who have created solutions for segregated or misrepresented populations. These efforts are attempting to counter and critique architecture practice as subservient to what Naomi Klein has called "Shock Capitalism,"[9] turning the gaze toward architecture engaging with the victims of dispossessions and populations left astray after ecological or financial disasters. As Christopher Hawthorne has framed it, the 2016 Venice Architecture Biennial established a critique to global real estate speculation, the expropriation of pools of collective knowledge and the monetization of common spaces by the so-called "sharing economy" of Uber and Airbnb.[10]

Both of the attitudes just described, formal exuberance for elite clients and the inevitable backlash in attempting to build an ethical high ground, are indeed the inevitable face of a neoliberal system. As Paul Mason reminds us,

> Capitalism is the Primark Factory that collapsed in Bangladesh and it is the rioting teenage girls at the opening of the Primark store in London, overexcited at the prospect of bargain clothes.[11]

FIGURE I.2 Architecture model of the Lewis Residence by Frank Gehry.

Source: Image Courtesy by Gehry Partners.

This "winner-takes-all" mentality operates in the edges of a bell curve. The center, or belly of the curve, has shrunk, disappeared or even worse, become uninteresting as a project for architecture. The belly of the bell curve is the bulk of the population, a middle class that occupies the bulk of the architecture of cities.

The body of professionals urgently needs to reclaim the authority to define a value for labor that is not dictated by the asymmetries of capital. A first step is to reject a tradition of subsidizing the avant-garde through free or underpaid labor. Progressive architecture has become synonymous with regressive social practices. This are systemic problems that are echoed in other fields. As reported by Ross Perlin in the years following the financial crisis, "[I]nternships are replacing untold numbers of full-time jobs: anecdotal evidence abounds of managers eliminating staff and using unpaid interns instead, and of organizations replacing paid internships with unpaid ones."[12] What is clear, as Paul Mason has framed it, is that this generation will not have the same opportunities as the previous one.[13]

Architecture production, at the beginning of the 21st century, reflects the polarization of the field; on one hand, there is a thriving field of research and practice that operates under ruthless competition where many actors are willing to work for free in order to "make it" into the star circle. On the other hand, there is a turn to austerity and "core" values of architecture that attempt to rectify the exploitations and dispossessions as a result of the economic order. While contradictory, both of these paths have become valid models of architectural practice, and it is not rare to see design firms practicing at both ends.

Reclaiming the middle

In 1914 Henry Ford decided to increase the minimum wage of workers to five US dollars a day, which equated to double the average wage of automakers at the time. Ford understood that the consumer power of his workers was linked to the industry he was trying to grow. As he explained,

> [T]he owner, the employees, and the buying public are all one and the same, and unless an industry can so manage itself as to keep wages high and prices low, it destroys itself, for otherwise, it limits the number of its customers. One's own employees ought to be one's own best customers.[14]

Ford was attempting to allow his workers to afford the cars they were building. Today, after accumulating considerable amounts of student debt, American architects cannot afford the type of architecture they are asked to design. The culture fostered by the "starchitect" system requires substantial subsidies coming from underpaid intern labor and exploitative practices. Even practices that engage with a social agenda have come to rely on the subsidy of free internships.[15] Young architects accept low-paying jobs to design one-of-a-kind buildings and exuberant furniture while they can only afford IKEA products. Isn't it possible to realign architects' design aspirations with the middle-class wage offered by our practice?

At the beginning of the 21st century, an architecture for the middle class seems to be driven by commercial imperatives. The central portion of the bell curve has often been associated with a market that is not in the hands of architects, what Rem Koolhaas calls "Junkspace."[16] Lacking the glamor of the bespoke or the heroism of a humanitarian aid, the middle has been rendered no longer valuable for the pursuits of the discipline. The field is still fearful to engage in larger narratives that are reminiscent of the modern movement. Perhaps there are avenues to develop a critical discourse and practice that does not operate outside or at the fringes of the market.

However, an economic deadlock produced by the extraction imperative[17] of the neoliberal agenda has forced a project of autonomy to emerge from self-provision. Architects can recast themselves as both users and producers of the architectures they envision, recalibrating the aspirations of design contributions to sustain and reconnect to the culture that they belong to.

The reclaiming of the middle does not imply a turn toward asceticism or austerity. Austerity has been an imposition from financial institutions to force governments to slice public services in order to pay debt, as opposed to the potential increase of taxes for the financial institutions that generated the problem in the first place. The term austerity has been a branding mechanism to persuade the population that after events like the 2008 financial crisis, governments will be expected to limit public spending, while banks will be bailed out. As explained by Randy Shaw, the housing crisis is an affordability problem: an increasing number of citizens can no longer afford to live in the places where they work.[18] It is necessary to establish a counterbalance to market speculation by both the public sector and by the Commons. Emerging movements founded on notions of collectivism can define a third leg of what traditionally has been a public/private duopoly.

This book advocates for the reclaiming of the middle and actively engages in the production of larger narratives that could rekindle a collaborative imagination. It hopes to invigorate the theorization of the collective and design practices that can define their own value system.

The post-2008 perspective

The 2008 financial crisis brought a new sense of awareness of how deep neoliberal economics has been accepted and perpetuated by both liberal and conservative governments and a creeping awareness that the system is not working in the majority's interests. The reality of the architectural discipline is that all architects are on the receiving end of an economic model that siphons value from the middle to the top. The year 2008 was a wake-up call to consider how the tools we architects use are in fact socio-technical systems that have an implicit economic agenda. Architectural form can no longer be disentangled from economic drives and motivations behind the capital that enables it.

From a socio-technical perspective, the weapon of choice of current economic practices has seen the rise of digital platforms as tools for the standardization of users and the extraction of capital. What Nick Srnicek has denominated "Platform

Capitalism"[19] or what Susana Zuboff has called "Surveillance Capitalism"[20] denounced the rise of platforms. Platforms are global organizations that operate as network providers, dictating the rules of interaction between users and profiting from the knowledge acquired by the monitoring of transactions on the platform. The rise of platforms has been accompanied by accentuated forms of economic inequality, as they offer novel ways to bypass market regulations.

In architecture, the architectural competition can be read as an embryonic platform, but perhaps a far more primitive and vicious one. The architectural competition also operates at a higher hierarchy, determining what does and does not constitute work worth remunerating. Competitions constitute a form of speculative work and have become mechanisms, as argued by Trebor Scholz, to bypass market regulations regarding employment, working hours and minimum wage.[21] Like Uber, competitions celebrate an architect entrepreneur who is his or her own boss and should wager the risk/reward to take part in a given call.

The 2008 financial crisis has started to work as an eye opener for a generation of architects that operates within architecture's very own speculative market. The first realization is that of belonging and understanding that we have accepted and celebrated a "winner-takes-all" economic system in the design work we so often do for free in the hope of recognition from a competition or another platform aggregator. The emerging No!Spec movement gives evidence of the uncanny realization that we have been engaging with unethical business practices, and it is necessary to design alternative models.[22] The financial crisis energized the rise of a resistance movement that can point out the consequences of unregulated markets, where speculative labor operates as a loophole that facilitates power asymmetry generating a structural divide and increasing inequality.

However, the 2008 crisis has also accelerated the production of alternatives, a socio-technical awareness that connects ideology with infrastructure that attempts to fabricate a different model. Such a model seeks for models of collective prosperity emphasizing the sovereignty of the labor practices we engage in. These include the creation of license agreements that can ensure the propagation of knowledge between users, as in the work of Richard Stallman with the General Purpose License and the copyleft movement; the creation of decentralized ledgers that can guarantee trust in a decentralized fashion, as in the advent of blockchain technology; and the design of Open Source forms of architecture that can empower users to self-provide dignified building solutions at affordable costs in the work of Alastair Parvin with the WikiHouse. This book is about such architectures. It is a socio-technical analysis of the infrastructures that are attempting to construct at different levels—ideological, tectonic, legal or computational—the rise of the Commons, as an independent and autonomous sphere of governance, one not predicated in the public/private dichotomy.

Framing architecture's Commons

This book is divided into five chapters. The first chapter, "Architectural progress," sets the foundation for a critique of architecture operating under neoliberal directives. The chapter questions that the notion of architectural progress has been in the service of citizens prosperity and examines how promises of ephemeralization, as advocated by Buckminster Fuller, have failed. Building on this, the argument put forward is that architectural progress hasn't been able to "trickle down" innovations to reach the general public. The chapter identifies how a neoliberal system operates through market enclosures, as is the case with intellectual property, benefiting from externalities, as is the case with poorly regulated labor and extracting value through surveillance mechanisms embedded in digital networks. The chapter makes the case that the value created by such a system is extracted from the Commons, dismantling provisions that define the power of the public domain. The Commons is framed through the writing of Elinor Ostrom, Antonio Negri and Michael Hardt, as well as the perspectives from David Bollier and Massimo De Angelis, attempting to gather a definition that encapsulates both material and immaterial Common-Pool Resources as well as the social structures that participate in the creation of collective wealth.

Chapter 2, "The coalescence of parts," dives deeper into how these extractive practices have been manifested in architecture. The chapter introduces a global manufacturing trend where the accumulation of capital has led to the rise of large manufacturing operations that exercise vertical integration, disrupting market diversity. The rise of vertical integration has offered clear innovations to manufacturing, by allowing a reduction of the number of parts that are necessary in technological assemblies. Recent technologies like 3-D printing have been able to offer performative advantages through the dissolution of previously standardized components. The trend toward vertical integration has a clear correlation with the paradigm of parametric design which is founded under a continuous model of mathematics. The chapter hopes to identify that the parametric model serves a narrow section of the population and has impacted market diversity.

Chapter 3, "In defense of parts," begins to put forward propositions for alternative design trajectories by understanding the social affordance of parts in design and manufacturing. It proposes that in order to sustain a diverse multi-actor economy, the field of architectural design needs to find efficient forms of collaboration and coordination between suppliers. While such efforts could be seen to have a correlation with institutions such as the Modular Society in the 1950s, as has been documented by Christine Wall, contemporary attempts seek to provide non-homogenizing frameworks of dimensional coordination through the advent of digital networks. The framework that is put forward is that of Discrete Architecture, where parts are designed and studied in their capacity for recombination and afford a multiplicity of outputs, a paradigm that lives in opposition to the "one-off" model offered by the continuous model of parametrics. Through Discrete Architecture, design is able to acknowledge the necessity to maintain a pluralistic and non-monopolistic approach to production. The benefits of the discrete agenda are examined through the study of the "combinatorial surplus" of parts and their affordance for the production of Design Commons. The chapter advocates for the adoption of combinatorial design, allowing for reusable patterns to be propagated through information networks.

Chapter 4, "Immaterial architectures," presents the argument that while network infrastructure has been utilized for the implementation of surveillance capitalism, it is possible to design and envision digital networks that do not exercise coercive power over its users. The chapter maps the challenges that platforms need to overcome to transition from being tools for extraction to tools for cooperation. This chapter revises ideas such as Platform Cooperativism as advocated by Trebor Scholz, who defines a core set of principles that allow digital networks to create wealth to the members of the network and not siphon it out. The chapter speculates further in the possibility of developing platforms for architecture that are able to aid in the collaboration between users, potentially generating repositories of Open Source architecture models that can serve the Commons. The technologies of videogames are analyzed as offering models for cooperation between players and a tradition of participation in digital communities.

It is necessary to theorize and conceptualize what should be expected from the successful implementation of these ideas. Chapter 5, "Reconstruction through self-provision," puts forward the argument that the Commons should seek to establish interpersonal freedoms that are grounded on ideas of diversity. The infrastructure developed by surveillance capitalism has effectively deployed intelligence generated from the aggregate data of users but obtained through illegitimate means. The Commons is argued to have the potential to reconstruct a form of consensual collective infrastructure that does not operate as a hierarchy. The chapter seeks to identify how we can embed democracy and oversight into technology, maintaining a level playing field and designing down the barrier of entry.

The ideas presented in this volume have been developed alongside design research in architecture by the studio Plethora Project. While many of the concepts and ideas presented throughout the book can be directly associated with Plethora Project's work, as can be seen through some of the figures, this volume has made a conscious attempt to expand on the ideas and go beyond what has been already achieved through design research, as often ideas move faster than their implementation. In this way this volume has become instrumental in operating as an ideological guideline for design, reminding us of the critical imperatives and opportunities that the field faces today.

Notes

1 Douglas Spencer, *The Architecture of Neoliberalism: How Contemporary Architecture Became an Instrument of Control and Compliance* (Bloomsbury Academic, 2016).
2 Mario Carpo, *The Second Digital Turn: Design Beyond Intelligence* (MIT Press, 2017).
3 Tim Jonze, 'Row Over Use of Unpaid Interns by Serpentine Pavilion Architect,' *The Guardian*, 2019 <www.theguardian.com/artanddesign/2019/mar/22/row-unpaid-interns-serpentine-london-gallery-pavilion-architect-project>.
4 Patrik Schumacher, *The Autopoiesis of Architecture, Volume II: A New Agenda for Architecture* (Wiley, 2012).

5 Schumacher, *The Autopoiesis of Architecture, Volume II: A New Agenda for Architecture*.

6 Patrik Schumacher, *The Autopoiesis of Architecture: A New Framework for Architecture* (Wiley, 2011).

7 Paul Goldberger, *Building Art: The Life and Work of Frank Gehry* (Random House, 2015).

8 Goldberger, *Building Art*.

9 Naomi Klein, *The Shock Doctrine: The Rise of Disaster Capitalism* (Metropolitan Books, 2010).

10 Christopher Hawthorne, 'A Grassroots, Handmade Venice Architecture Biennale from Alejandro Aravena,' *Los Angeles Times*, 2016 <www.latimes.com/entertainment/arts/la-et-cm-venice-biennale-review-20160530-snap-story.html>.

11 Paul Mason, *Postcapitalism: A Guide to Our Future* (Farrar, Straus and Giroux, 2016).

12 Ross Perlin, *Intern Nation: How to Earn Nothing and Learn Little in the Brave New Economy* (Verso, 2012).

13 Mason, *Postcapitalism*.

14 Jeff Nilsson, 'Why Did Henry Ford Double His Minimum Wage?,' 2014 <www.saturdayeveningpost.com/2014/01/03/history/post-perspective/ford-doubles-minimum-wage.html>.

15 India Block, 'Elemental Ends Internships amid Growing Row Over Unpaid Work in Architecture Studios,' 2019 <www.dezeen.com/2019/03/27/elemental-unpaid-internships-row/>.

16 Rem Koolhaas, *Content* (Taschen, 2004).

17 Shoshana Zuboff, *The Age of Surveillance Capitalism: The Fight for a Human Future at the New Frontier of Power* (PublicAffairs, 2019).

18 Randy Shaw, *Generation Priced Out: Who Gets to Live in the New Urban America* (University of California Press, 2018).

19 Nick Srnicek, *Platform Capitalism* (Polity, 2017).

20 Zuboff, *The Age of Surveillance Capitalism*.

21 Trebor Scholz, 'Digital Labor: New Opportunities, Old Inequalities,' *Re:Publica 2013*, 2013 <www.youtube.com/watch?v=52CqKIR0rVM>.

22 David Airey, 'No!Spec,' 1997 <www.nospec.com/> [accessed 10 October 2015].

References

Airey, David, 'No!Spec,' 1997 <www.nospec.com/> [accessed 10 October 2015]

Aureli, Pier Vittorio, *Less Is Enough: On Architecture and Asceticism* (Strelka Press, Moscow, 2013)

Block, India, 'Elemental Ends Internships Amid Growing Row Over Unpaid Work in Architecture Studios,' 2019 <www.dezeen.com/2019/03/27/elemental-unpaid-internships-row/> [accessed 07 July 2019]

Carpo, Mario, *The Second Digital Turn: Design Beyond Intelligence* (Massachusetts Institute of Technology Press, Cambridge, 2017)

Goldberger, Paul, *Building Art: The Life and Work of Frank Gehry* (Penguin Random House, New York, 2015)

Hawthorne, Christopher, 'A Grassroots, Handmade Venice Architecture Biennale from Alejandro Aravena,' *Los Angeles Times*, 2016 <www.latimes.com/entertainment/arts/la-et-cm-venice-biennale-review-20160530-snap-story.html> [accessed 12 July 2019]

Jonze, Tim, 'Row Over Use of Unpaid Interns by Serpentine Pavilion Architect,' *The Guardian*, 2019 <www.theguardian.com/artanddesign/2019/mar/22/row-unpaid-interns-serpentine-london-gallery-pavilion-architect-project> [accessed 12 July 2019]

Klein, Naomi, *The Shock Doctrine: The Rise of Disaster Capitalism* (Metropolitan Books, New York, 2010)

Koolhaas, Rem, *Content* (Taschen, London, 2004)

Mason, Paul, *Postcapitalism: A Guide to Our Future* (Farrar, Straus and Giroux, New York, 2016)

Nilsson, Jeff, 'Why Did Henry Ford Double His Minimum Wage?,' 2014 <www.saturdayeveningpost.com/2014/01/03/history/post-perspective/ford-doubles-minimum-wage.html> [accessed 21 November 2018]

Perlin, Ross, *Intern Nation: How to Earn Nothing and Learn Little in the Brave New Economy* (Verso, London, New York, 2012)

Scholz, Trebor, 'Digital Labor: New Opportunities, Old Inequalities,' *Re:Publica 2013*, 2013 <www.youtube.com/watch?v=52CqKIR0rVM> [accessed 12 September 2017]

Schumacher, Patrik, *The Autopoiesis of Architecture: A New Framework for Architecture* (Wiley, Chichester, 2011)

———, *The Autopoiesis of Architecture, Volume II: A New Agenda for Architecture* (Wiley, Chichester, 2012)

Shaw, Randy, *Generation Priced Out: Who Gets to Live in the New Urban America* (University of California Press, Oakland, 2018)

Spencer, Douglas, *The Architecture of Neoliberalism: How Contemporary Architecture Became an Instrument of Control and Compliance* (Bloomsbury Academic, London and New York, 2016)

Srnicek, Nick, *Platform Capitalism* (Polity Press, Cambridge, 2017)

Zuboff, Shoshana, *The Age of Surveillance Capitalism: The Fight for a Human Future at the New Frontier of Power* (PublicAffairs, New York, 2019)

1

ARCHITECTURAL PROGRESS

While the 1990s were a time for experimentation, delineating all the possible trajectories that architecture could take in the advent of computational technologies, the beginning of the 21st century has been marked by an actual realization of ideas that seemed inconceivable three decades ago. Architecture has experienced a time of incredible innovation. The advancements of the discipline are plentiful and in all areas of expertise. The computer has been adopted by the field to the point that it's difficult to distinguish between digital and traditional practice. The discipline seems to be reinventing its possibilities at an incredibly accelerated rate.

Digital fabrication and robotic manufacturing has become a large field of research within the discipline, allowing for computer numeric control (CNC) manufacturing to profoundly alter the notion of seriality and customization in design. The blobs that occupied the virtual space seen through architects' screens for many years have today been rationalized and fabricated. The development of software infrastructure that aids in the rationalization and construction of complex geometries has grown exponentially, opening a pathway for architects to become creators of the tools that they use. Parametric and BIM software have effectively been able to allow the accurate modeling of buildings, integrating systems and allow for associative geometries. Simulation has allowed the calculation of a building's energy efficiency and sunlight penetration, anticipating the performance and perception of space prior to its construction. Data collection from completed buildings enabled the improvement of existing energy efficiency models and circulation diagrams that can anticipate the movement of people within a building. At a micro scale, material science has allowed for the creation of "digital materials" that can be engineered in its translucency and flexibility. Software tools can be used to model matter in its molecular composition and not just as a boundary representation of a solid. Composites allow for shells of minimal weight that use the directionality of fibers to calculate and resist large weight load. Today, the pursuit of efficiency turns toward automation and artificial intelligence as technologies that can fundamentally redefine labor practices.

The historic trajectory of innovation has allowed architects such as Patrik Schumacher to argue for a vector of progress in the gradual implementation of new geometric principles in architecture.[1] For Schumacher, innovations in architectural geometry allow for new forms of order that in turn allow for framing and ordering social processes. What can be understood from Schumacher's writings is a sense that architectural progress is associated with the formal and geometrical freedoms allowed by technological innovations.[2]

Architectural progress currently exists, as argued by Schumacher, as a self-sufficient autopoietic system, one that seems to operate autonomously from any correlation with the market, other disciplines or any social contingency. Schumacher argues that "Parametricism" or "Tectonism," his proposed terminology for a 21st century hegemonical style, proposes architectural innovations on two fronts:

> Parametricism's radical ontological and methodological innovation translates into a massive leap in both dimensions of architectural progress considered here; i.e., it entails an unprecedented expansion of architecture's compositional freedom and versatility and an unprecedented leap in architecture's ordering capacity through the deployment of algorithms and associative logics.[3]

The compositional freedom that Schumacher describes follows a series of simple heuristics where malleable fluid forms interpolate between requirements, a formal organization structure that uses curves as a form of negotiation. The result of this "articulation" is the production of gradients that eliminate discreteness and autonomy between elements, resulting in the coalescence of larger wholes. Repetitive elements are to be avoided in favor of larger gestures that integrate layers of structural and performative requirements.

An autopoietic progress has been argued to be an emergent property of technology itself, defining an autonomous self-preserving pursuit of innovation.[4] In a similar way, the introduction of the term autopoiesis in architecture attempts to define a disciplinary boundary and an internal code and value system with the purpose of its self production. Architectural progress can therefore be identified as an autonomous practice of architecture that seeks the advancement of a formal and conceptual repertoire of an architectural vocabulary.

Architectural progress becomes an end in itself, as it declares that the ultimate pursuit of the discipline is for the production of novelty, independent of its capacity to be effectively implemented in the world. Knowledge and creativity become a powerful commodity, as they encapsulate architecture's value proposition, one of willingness to reinvent itself perpetually. The mechanism that is in charge of allowing innovation to permeate and reach society at large is that of "trickle down economics," a theory that suggests that all innovation should happen in service of the most ambitious clients and that over time such innovation will make its way to the general public.

The narrative of "trickle-down economics" has become an alibi to pursue design commissions for the richest 1% of clients, obscuring the inability of the practice to contribute to a larger societal agenda. The scarcity of clients that can effectively engage with such definition of architectural progress naturally generates an aggressive competition between peers. The scarcity of commissions can be understood as resulting from the value system that the discipline has forged, one that is at odds with the market and the public. It is in this way that architecture has manufactured a structural improbability for success, celebrating elusive commissions that somehow manage to defy market logic. Architecture progress, in its current form, requires a form of subsidy, often fulfilled by philanthropy, free labor or wealthy clients with a unique understanding of the discipline.

Ephemeralization fails

The pursuit of innovation and architectural progress has historically been linked to optimistic narratives. In 1938, architect, theorist and futurist R. Buckminster Fuller in his book *Nine Chains to the Moon* introduced the term "ephemeralization" to describe how technological advancements trend toward allowing designers to do "more with less."[5] Fuller sees designers as having the capacity to radically change the expectations of the market via disruptive innovations. As he framed it:

> There is not a chapter in any book of economics anywhere about doing more with less. Economists traditionally try to maximize what you have, but the idea that you could go from wire to wireless or from visible structuring to invisible alloy structuring did not occur to them at all. It was outside their point of view—beyond their range of vision.[6]

Fuller calculates the ratio between the weight or mass of materials and their capacity for action (such as structural performance), establishing a metric of progress and a trajectory toward ever more ephemeral or lighter building blocks for society and culture. For Fuller, when examined as a global trend, ephemeralization proposed a narrative where design and technology lead toward prosperity. This ultimately allows for the finite resources available on our planet to be optimized for access by the rest of the population. Doing more with less was equated with more for the many.

As argued by Peter Joseph,[7] the concept of ephemeralization can be closely linked with Jeremy Rifkin's claim for how capitalism reduces the cost of products and services toward zero. Rifkin's concept of zero marginal cost[8] is the process in which the initial costs of industrialization and innovation are distributed through the products or value produced by any system. This results in making every copy of a product cheaper than the previous copy, i.e., a descending curve trending toward zero. Examples like computer technology are used by Rifkin to demonstrate an economic trajectory where the initial investment could be considered negligible in relation to the value produced over time. For Rifkin, the trajectory toward zero

FIGURES 1.1 AND 1.2 Buckminster Fuller holding up tensegrity sphere. Tensegrity demonstrates his principle of ephemeralization, where structural stability is achieved with fewer materials.

Source: Images Courtesy by The Estate of R. Buckminster Fuller

marginal costs defines the road map toward the eclipse of capitalism, allowing for a new economic system to emerge in its place.

While the narrative of ephemeralization through optimization and technological innovation can on paper be seen as a contributor toward prosperity, the beginning of the 21st century has exhibited an acute growth of economic inequality, as argued and demonstrated by the research of Thomas Piketty.[9] The development of inequality would therefore suggest that innovation and the capacity of doing more with less disproportionally benefits a few over others. Piketty states that the rate of return in capital (as in wealth) is larger than the rate growth of the economy (as in labor). This creates a trend where over time, inequality increases. Trickle-down economics, therefore, aiming to provide with innovation at the very top of the pyramid, disproportionately benefits those who already play with an economic advantage. Ephemeralization fails not through its capacity to do more with less but through its capacity to distribute its innovations on economic efficiency to the population.

As has been argued by Pier Vittorio Aureli, increases in performance and efficiency in production can be coupled with a perpetual necessity for creativity. For Aureli, these are central features of our current capitalist system, one that has managed to manufacture scarcity. Aureli argues that capitalist culture has always tried to obtain more with less. Aureli presents technology as a mechanism by which capitalists are able to fulfil the very notion of industry, writing that "to be industrious means being able to obtain the best results with fewer means."[10] Aureli goes further by pointing out that creativity, as the most generic faculty of human life, is sought by capital to be exploited as its main labor power. He states:

> [I]n an economic crisis, what capital's austerity measures demand is that people do more with less: more work for less money, more creativity with less social security. In this context, the principle of "less is more" runs the risk of becoming a cynical celebration of the ethos of austerity and budget cuts to social programmes.[11]

From Aureli's perspective, it appears that Fuller's ephemeralization is bound to play into the hands of capitalist production, offering cost-reducing opportunities for wealth accumulation. Aureli's position fails to acknowledge that not all production is equal; more with less can result in an extractive practice if imposed by a hierarchical actor but can also result in an emancipatory strategy from grassroots organizations. Self-production, as we will explore later in this volume, is able to break free from market logic and from external impositions of asceticism, especially in the manifestation of local values.

Winner-takes-all

The current globalized economic system systematically privileges the rise of the few, generating wealthy oligopolies. You do not need to live in a third-world country today to be a precarious worker.[12] This "winner-takes-all" mentality has contributed to the current establishment of a "star" system of architects, and the impoverishment of a larger sector of the discipline, which in its continuous attempt to jump into the boat of the 1%, persists in unethical labor practices.

While architectural competitions have been a long-standing tradition in the practice of architecture, the rise of architectural competitions at the end of the

20th century, accelerated by digital technologies, has become a mechanism for the exploitation of creativity. Architecture competitions have today become a central mechanism for the allocation of capital for architectural projects. Through open calls for participation, hundreds and sometimes thousands of architectural firms contribute free labor to take part in proposing a design, often without the certainty that there are funds available for it to be executed if the competition is won. The risk-vs-reward ratio presented by the competition model is very simple: winner takes all. While the chances to win are slim, the reward, in contrast, can become an instant ticket to stardom.

There certainly are many motivations for architects to take part in architectural competitions. The opportunity to develop a portfolio and contribute to architectural discourse through design proposals that can be evaluated side by side at a particular point in time are typical motivations. However, these are trumped by the asymmetry of power established between those who have capital and those seeking an opportunity for labor. The capital incentive generates a behavioral blindness, where any form of cooperation is disregarded. The result of this operation is incredibly inefficient, able to brute-force itself through design alternatives. Moreover, current formats for competitions are not regulated or incentivized to contribute to a repository of collective public knowledge, ideas that might formalize some societal or disciplinary public wealth from their exercise.

Competitions have been denounced by architects and institutions such as the Architecture Lobby as unfair mechanisms of exploitation that undervalue professional labor.[13] The Architecture Lobby has gone much further than just denouncing exploitative labor practices: it has called for unionization of architects and developed guidelines for good labor practices in the discipline.[14]

Architectural competition's international outreach has grown using digital platforms facilitating participation, therefore optimizing value extraction. In his studies of digital labor, Trebor Scholz states that competitions operate as a form of crowdsourcing, a contemporary technique that is able to further extract free capital from pools of workers.[15] No official contract is present in a competition call, so no minimum wage or social security applies.[16]

The recent rise of tech giants such as Google, Facebook and Amazon have further contributed to the rise of economic inequality. While the Internet was initially understood as a promising infrastructure that would democratize access and level the playing field, today, as has been argued by Shoshana Zuboff, it has become dominated by a wealth extraction imperative.[17] Millions of people have been able to gain access to new information, define a marketplace for their production or even depend on forms of labor that have emerged from digital transactions, but market dominance between a few network providers demonstrates that all the "free" infrastructure that has been provided has come at an incredibly high cost.

The economic model and value system in which architects operate is not dissociated from global trends. The maximization of profits and "winner-takes-all" mentality has become the operating system for economic activity. It has become necessary for architecture to develop an internal critique and an assessment of how some of its practices are complicit in the rise of asymmetries and models of innovation that will never reach any societal value. In order to move away from "winner-takes-all," we first need to clearly identify the mechanisms that contribute to the perpetuation of neoliberalism.

Architecture in the face of neoliberalism: extractivism, externalities and enclosures

The practice of architecture cannot be disentangled from the capital that allows for architecture to be built or practiced. The current practice of neoliberal economics is characterized by strong deregulation and privatization of public infrastructure. We will use the studies of economist Joseph Stiglitz, scholar Shoshana Zuboff and economist Mariana Mazzucato to identify three mechanisms that advance the asymmetric growth of the economy: extractivism, externalities and enclosures. Each one of these terms encapsulates commonplace practices of neoliberal culture.

Extractivism is the practice of obtaining value through value extraction or what we associate with rent, where wealth accumulation allows for the extraction of capital without the production of value. As framed by Mazzucato:

> "Rent-seeking" here refers to the attempt to generate income, not by producing anything new but by overcharging above the "competitive price," and undercutting competition by exploiting particular advantages (including labour), or, in the case of an industry with large firms, their ability to block other companies from entering that industry, thereby retaining a monopoly advantage.[18]

Extractivism also refers to the practice of collecting unregulated assets, as is the case with user data in digital platforms or free labor through speculative work. Zuboff goes further and explains how tech companies today operate under an "extraction imperative," one that leaves behind the 20th-century industrial capitalism that produced economies of scale in order to produce low unit cost. Her definition of surveillance capitalism, the neoliberal practices of tech giants, demand the extraction of behavioral data, which is transformed into predictions for accurate targeting.[19]

Extractivism presents a first challenge to architecture both internally through the way we organize and define ethical labor practices and in terms of architectural output, an appreciating asset that is transferred to the real-estate market. Architects might argue that both the input, in terms of capital, and the output, in terms of the ownership of the property, is completely outside the domain of the discipline, but it's precisely that disciplinary boundary that locks us into neoliberal economics, as it is possible not only to consider innovation in tectonics but also in ownership and fundraising strategies.

The second idea is that of externalities. Mazzucato explains that within marginal utility theory, the market model classifies what is considered productive and unproductive.[20] Negative externalities are the consequences of a productive operation.

Here, the calculation of costs is only done internally, within what is included in the production boundary. The societal cost or consequences of an operation are not considered. For example, it is cheaper not to include the cost associated with the impact to the environment. The exploitation of negative externalities takes advantage of an unregulated condition or lack of public awareness of the side effects of the event. Here again, a venture will stall and fight against any regulation that would imply an increase in cost for the enterprise.

The challenge of externalities is associated with defining an economic model that cannot be exploited by corporations and resisting the eradication of values, such as cultural heritage, that often is not considered within economic practice. The definition of what should be included within an economic model is a constant social struggle in the attempt to reach legislation that can provide regulation or taxation for the exploitation of externalities, as has been discussed with the notion of a carbon tax. But it is possible also to observe how architecture projects can bring ecological awareness and address the issues of externalities as central to the discourse. It is also possible, as we will discuss in the following chapters, how to produce positive externalities that aim to contribute to societal wealth.

Finally, enclosures refer to the practice of privatization of what otherwise would belong to the public domain or to the Commons. While enclosures were originally applied to land, today the challenge has migrated more and more toward copyrights and intellectual property. The key strategy behind enclosures is to block access to a given resource or knowledge in order to profit from its demand. Stiglitz uses the term "moat," originally used by Warren Buffett, to describe the entry barrier designed by companies to avoid free competition. As he explains:

> [T]here has been a great deal of innovation in the creation, leveraging, and preservation of market power—in the tools that managers use to increase the moat that surrounds them and with which they can use the resulting power to exploit others and increase their profits. It is understandable why our business leaders don't like competition: competition drives profits down, to the point at which firms receive a return on their capital at a level that is just enough to sustain keeping investment in the business, taking into account its risk. They seek higher profits than that which a competitive market would afford—hence the necessity of building bigger moats to forestall competition and the enormous innovation in doing so.[21]

Stiglitz further explains how the extension of the life of copyrights allows companies to maintain market power and avoid competition. This generates friction and limits the free flow of knowledge.[22] Architecture is a discipline with great demands for capital, therefore presenting a high barrier of entry. While certification and regulation can be argued to increase the barrier of entry, this volume will focus mainly on how to reduce it, by strategies of knowledge propagation and distributed practices for architectural literacy.

The value obtained from the practice of extractivism, externalities and enclosures (EEE), though it appears to be only monetary value, is also the value of the

Commons. The practice of EEE represents an attack of the Commons, a sphere that describes societal value (material and immaterial) beyond market logic. It is in the protection and construction of the Commons through design that this book will spend most of its energy in the following chapters, but first it is important to provide a framework to understand the Commons.

The Commons

Before the advent of private property, the term "Commons" indicated the natural resources that were freely accessible to society as a collective. Pastures, minerals, forests and so on constituted the wealth of societies and could be exploited by anyone. Today, the notion of Commons has evolved to include not only natural resources but also any wealth that is available to a collective. The term also has largely been understood to refer not only to material or immaterial resources but also to the social systems surrounding their administration, protection and production.

As argued by Garret Hardin in 1968 with his paper "The Tragedy of the Commons,"[23] the Commons suffer from the possibility of unorganized exploitation that inevitably leads toward depletion or ruination of shared resources. Hardin explained his rationale through a thought experiment where many farmers, motivated by self-interest, would exploit a pasture to its ruin in order to grow their herds. As argued by David Bollier,[24] Hardin's argument was used to defend the rise of private property and legal inheritance as a mechanism for the administration of land.

The Tragedy of the Commons has been analyzed thoroughly by economists. As presented by Nobel Laureate in Economics Elinor Ostrom, the most common analysis of Hardin's tragedy thesis is an assimilation of it with a prisoner's dilemma game.[25] Belonging to the field of game theory, a prisoner's dilemma game is a hypothetical puzzle that attempts to predict the rational behavior of economic actors. As Ostrom explains, a prisoner dilemma is a noncooperative game in which two prisoners with no ability to communicate need to take decisions based on a payoff matrix. The outcome of each prisoner is not only dependent on their own action, but also on the action of the other prisoner. The game has been greatly utilized to demonstrate how rational individuals can generate irrational collective behavior.

For Ostrom, the Tragedy of the Commons is only possible under the assumption that the prisoners are indeed prisoners, unable to change or design the rules of their potential cooperation. She challenges and denounces the use of the tragedy model as a means to validate centralized governments or private property rights. As she describes it:

> Both centralization advocates and privatization advocates accept as a central tenet that institutional change must come from outside and be imposed on the individuals affected.[26]

Ostrom's Nobel Prize in 2009 comes with critical timing. Her studies of the Commons reemphasize the need of study of the governing structures for "Common-Pool Resources" (CPRs). Her case studies of communities that require self-organizing structures to allow collective access to scarce physical resources are extremely relevant in light of the 2008 recession.

Herein lies the difficulty to fully grasp the Commons as a term and as a frame for action. On the one hand, we have Ostrom's approach to understand CPRs: these are material resources that historically belong to collectives, such as fish, minerals or forests. While Ostrom performs most of her analysis in material resources and the communities surrounding them, the idea of CPRs can also be applied to immaterial goods, such as knowledge or digital assets. This is what Massimo De Angelis calls "Common Goods," goods that are of the value and use of a plurality.[27]

As Bollier points out, when we shift from talking about the resources themselves to the governing social structures that administrate them, we speak of the "Commons."[28] Here we would understand the Commons also as social systems and not only as repositories of wealth. For the Commons to exist, as argued by De Angelis, there needs to be plurality or community of commoners that claim ownership of a common good.[29] It is precisely this social system that defeats and falsifies the notion of the Tragedy of the Commons, as the social governing structures that protect common goods also ensure that they do not get overexploited. This is a process of cooperation and coordination. As an example, we can think of Commons as the self-governing rulesets and constraints that fishermen in certain communities use to ensure a sustainable exploitation of the sea, or the self-organizing contributors of public digital infrastructure such as Wikipedia.

Finally, authors such as Antonio Negri and Michael Hardt utilize the term "the Common" to describe both CPRs and the governing structures that ensure their democratic access. They place emphasis in the philosophical underpinnings of such enterprise as a form of social production. As a response to neoliberal extractivism, Negri and Hardt share an urgent call together with many of the citizens and intellectuals to reformulate "The Common." The Common, is a term that encapsulates a series of ideas that is important to untangle. As they explain:

> The common is defined first, then, in contrast to property, both private and public. It is not a new form of property but rather nonproperty, that is, a fundamentally different means of organizing the use and management of wealth. The common designates an equal and open structure for access to wealth together with democratic mechanisms of decision-making. More colloquially, one might say that the common is what we share or, rather, it is a social structure and a social technology for sharing.[30]

The decision to denominate "the Common" as such emerges as an attempt to differentiate from, and reinvigorate, the legacy challenge of "the Commons." As they explain:

> The common we share, in fact, is not so much discovered as it is produced. (We are reluctant call this the commons because that term refers to precapitalist-shared spaces that were destroyed by the advent of private property.

Although more awkward, "the common" highlights the philosophical content of the term and emphasizes that this is not a return to the past but a new
development.)[31]

Negri and Hardt's definition understands the Common as a concept of non-property
that applies to social wealth. De Angelis echoes the notion of non-property establishing a difference between capital and wealth. For De Angelis, economists look at
material and immaterial resources as capital. This includes the infrastructure to run
a factory or the money in the bank, as well as social networks in the form of social
capital and skills in the form of human capital. His move to denominate common
resources as wealth accentuates a distinction where accumulation is not pursuing
monetary enrichment. The wealth produced mediated by communing structures
he defines as "commonwealth."[32]

Negri and Hardt identify the Common as a constituency that needs to be identified outside the public/private dialectic. The Common rises as a third sphere
of action, one that should be considered autonomous from its public and private
counterpart. As Tiziana Terranova presents it:

> What is at stake for Antonio Negri and Michael Hardt is the reinvention of
> the "Common" as a constituent social relation, providing an alternative to
> both state and capital, public and private. Their notion of the common tries
> to avoid an identification of the common with the "natural commons" and
> instead develop a notion of immaterial commons such as education, research,
> health, and the production of life as such. In a financialized economy, this also
> means the desire to invent a new type of money, a "currency of the com-
> mon," expressing the powers of the multitudes rather than those of capital.[33]

Under this perspective, framing the project of architecture from the perspective
of the Commons establishes clear economic and social imperatives. It discusses who
benefits from economic or social progress. It removes the emphasis on vacuous
innovation and replaces it with a collective project for social wealth and prosperity.
Design and architecture, like every other discipline, will have a role to play in the
reconstruction of the Commons, after their decimation by neoliberal practices, and
it might require that we assess the boundaries of the discipline and the hierarchical
role we have granted to specific value systems that have placed emphasis on uneq-
uitable societal values.

For the purpose of this book, we will establish a distinction between CPRs or
Common Goods, the Commons and the Common, allowing us to clearly identify
the collective resources, their governing social structures, and the philosophical
implications of their construction. The call to reassess the Commons is linked to
its protection and reconstruction. The problem of market enclosures can therefore be reframed as an attack on the sovereignty of the Commons. In the past,
this struggle would have been understood through the protection and regulation
of access to natural resources, but today the battle is far more evident in issues of

intellectual property or the harvesting of data and value allowed by digital platforms. As argued by Negri and Hardt, this problem needs to be understood from a post-Fordist perspective. This allows for recognizing that today productive activity does not only occur in the factory but throughout all social interactions, blurring the line between leisure and work. Contemporary extractivist technologies are able to quantify and capitalize the totality of a digital footprint that individuals have come to assume they don't have any ownership or jurisdiction over.[34]

In architecture the Commons have mainly been addressed by the right for public space with all its political potentialities. In this book, the Commons will be presented and argued from a perspective closer to the labor that designers engage with, as well as the value, knowledge and expertise that live in the networks of education, ideation, collaboration and development, even if buildings do not reach materialization.

Architecture's Commons

The thesis of this volume is that by framing architecture's agenda through the perspective of the Commons, it is possible to recalibrate the role of design, generating awareness of its complicit contribution to neoliberal economics. The central argument is that design can create positive externalities: a surplus of value that, while perhaps not monetary, can certainly contribute to the reconstruction of the Commons. The result of fortifying the Commons would in turn, result in the reduction of the barrier of entry for new designers, increase education and literacy both of architects and the public, increase collaboration and reduce exploitation in the form of free labor.

The practice of architecture suffered a pivotal turn toward individual exploration since the failure of larger narratives present in the modern period. As Reinier de Graaf reminds us, Koolhass's "City of The Captive Globe" recognizes a condition of architecture where each plot is considered its own manifesto:

> After The City of the Captive Globe, architecture exists only in the plural, suggesting an apex of multiple choice. Formerly absolute ideologies are confined to the walls of their facades; their validity is limited to the boundary of their plots. Their simple coexistence within a single territory makes them relative; each vision cancels out the validity of the next. In The City of the Captive Globe architecture has agreed to disagree.[35]

De Graaf argues how modernist narratives failed in their attempts to unify. The pursuit of standardization and industrialization of architecture were part of postwar efforts to generate a collective consensus. The research of Christine Wall analyzing the project of "Dimensional Coordination" or "Modular Coordination" pursued by the Modular Society in the 1950s demonstrates an effort establish protocols of collaboration in order to seek reduction of waste and improve building efficiency.[36] This would be achieved by developing a unified system of components that could be reduced to a universal grid. These efforts focused for many years in agreeing on what would be the fundamental module; i.e., the smallest unit that would dictate a system of coordinates.

Any project of standardization suggests a degree of coordination, establishing agreements across the market. While maintaining competition, standardization suggests that there are mutual benefits from agreeing module sizes. The Modular Society was attempting to put in practice an economy of scale, where unit cost can be reduced by their serialization. The challenge they had to face was not the economics but rather the totalizing nature of their agenda when it comes to living.

Standardization and modular coordination constructed a narrative of efficiency and would propel innovation and technical development. There was an implicit intention of homogenization, which became a central argument of critique for architectural movements to come. The research in digital architecture, even today, is centered on the differentiation and mass customization of building elements, rejecting any form of standardization. Nevertheless, the question that arises today, specially when revisiting efforts of dimensional coordination, is if it is possible to conceive of collaborative forms of production and coordination between different economic actors without the totalizing and homogenizing principles established by the Modular Society.

Here is where the Commons intersects architectural thinking, as the challenge of the Common as argued by Negri and Hardt, as well as Professor Stavros Stavrides, is to define forms of collaboration that are not based in a process of homogenization but rather in a process of multiplicity.[37]

The Commons in the age of the Internet

Today we operate in a networked information economy. The Internet has become a place for the creation and propagation of knowledge. As argued by Yochai Benkler, a Harvard University law professor, in an information economy the physical capital for production is distributed throughout society. This means that the barrier of entry for creative or collaborative enterprises drops dramatically as individuals already possess the capital capacity for participation.[38] This departs from the legacy condition where capital requirements limited the capacity of individuals and collectives to contribute through creative endeavors.

Yet architecture has not radically changed since the introduction of network infrastructure. Structural changes in the practice of architecture utilizing digital networks are still to come. This places architecture at a critical advantage that will enable it to avoid the same mistakes made by other fields, where network infrastructure has been used as an extractive practice.

Architecture construction still depends on capital, due to material requirements, and perhaps even more importantly, dependence on land. Nevertheless, architectural knowledge and skill development, as well as the field's disciplinary and cultural capital, have the potential of utilizing information networks to reduce barriers of entry and democratize access to the discourse.

The content generated by users on the Internet provides a new form of social production that operates with its own set of values. As argued by Tiziana Terranova, the creation of value from social networks is not measured by the metric of labor, yet it is today driving financial capital.[39] The digital platform emerged at the turn of the 21st century as a piece of technological infrastructure that was able to standardize the involuntary contribution of thousands of individuals. Establishing a hierarchical relation with their users, platforms are able to dictate rules of engagement and define interactions in a format that is conducive for exploitation. Through digital platforms, individuals are unintentionally participating in the largest effort to coordinate user communications under a standardized protocol. Grand narratives are here, yet they are invisible under the propaganda of individual freedom.

Platforms like Uber encourage workers to think of themselves as liberated workers, owners of their own business or even as entrepreneurs able to design their own lifestyle and income structures. As Christian Marazzi points out, this move toward the externalization of labor has been a progressive method of increasing productivity by outsourcing production processes to users. This externalization of value production is demonstrated in the consumer-as-producer phenomenon, where companies like IKEA are able to externalize production by asking the consumer to identify the code of a product, locate the product, load and transport and finally assemble the product. As Marazzi explains, "The consumer contributes to market creation, producing services, managing damages, and hazards, sorting litter, optimizing the fixed assets of suppliers and even administration."[40]

For Marazzi, the implications of this massive expropriation of value goes beyond capital gains and the production of inequality. He defines such expropriations as a form of structural economic violence where value extraction decimates societal values not categorized by the economic model. He expands:

> These crowdsourcing strategies, leaching vital resources from the multitudes, represent the new organic composition of capital, the relationship between constant capital dispersed throughout society and variable capital as the whole of society, emotions, desires, relational capacities and a lot of "free labor" (unpaid labor), a quality that is despatialized as well, dispersed in the sphere of consumption and reproduction of the forms of life, of individual and collective imaginary.[41]

Crowdsourcing platforms, in the current form, extract from the Commons. By formalizing and integrating the Commons in our design and economic discourse, we no longer regard it as an externality or an unclaimed or underregulated resource free for the taking.

Architecture platforms

Architectural competitions are the closest model that the architecture discipline has developed to implement extractive practices. This can be understood as a form of platform exploitation, as the production of value will always more greatly benefit the network than those who produce the labor. Through a reading of David Harvey, architectural theorist Peggy Deamer recognizes the condition of entrepreneurialism of this new "gig economy" as a form of propaganda used by neoliberal practices that place a positive spin on crowdsourced operations. She explains:

> The contemporary conditions—flexibility, autonomy, entrepreneurialism—are those handed us by neo-liberalism, and it exploits all the conditions associated with immateriality. Harvey has pointed out that the neo-liberal agenda "can best be advanced by liberating individual entrepreneurial freedoms and skills within an institutional framework characterized by strong private property rights, free markets, and free trade."[42]

Adding to this idea, Pier Vittorio Aureli detects that in the early 20th century, Le Corbusier's Maison Dom-Ino model establishes a model that externalizes architectural production. As he presents it:

> [T]he best embodiment of this model for dwelling is Le Corbusier's Maison Dom-Ino (1914), a simple structural concrete framework that could be built by the inhabitants themselves with minimal resources and filled in according to their means. And yet, the very goal of the Dom-Ino model was to provide the lower classes with a minimum property that would allow them to become entrepreneurs of their own household condition.[43]

The reading of the Dom-Ino model as infrastructure for "Do-It-Yourself" (DIY) can be more explicitly seen in the work of Pritzker Prize winner Alejandro Aravena, who in his housing project Elemental decided to spend the government's social housing budget in providing half a house that could be further expanded by the inhabitants. For Aravena, this is an outcome that is the result of the available capital for public projects and his understanding of what should be the minimal ethical household. The force of neoliberalism here is not direct in the externalization of work expected by the architect but rather in the structural conditions that have led to a social housing budget not being enough for a complete house. But is important to distinguish who benefits from practices of distributed social production and DIY initiatives. Under digital platforms, all value produced is syphoned by the network. Aravena's model operates, as we will discuss later, as a form of self-provision, where the value of citizens remains in their hands. This is critical for social production to be able to contribute to the Commons, as opposed to being an extractive practice, as seen with architectural competitions.

Nevertheless, material infrastructure provided for citizens is not enough for a project like Elemental to succeed in the contribution to the Commons, as the networks of knowledge, cooperation and governance cannot be imposed within an architectural proposal. Aravena's model emphasizes the role of private property and individual self-production, providing empty spaces with clear demarcations of

FIGURE 1.3 Quinta Monroy, Elemental by Alejandro Aravena. The initial construction is later completed by homeowners.

Source: Image Courtesy by Elemental.

ownership. For Commons to emerge, it is necessary for citizens, commoners, to participate in the construction of codes and collective governance. Such negotiations and coordination, are imperative, as argued by Ostrom,[44] to avoid the Tragedy of the Commons.

The idea of "self-provision," where citizens are able to utilize both material and immaterial local resources to establish new relations of autonomy and cooperation, calls for reclamation of the concept of entrepreneur. This would allow citizens to dedicate their efforts in a form of resistance and autonomy rather than in an orchestrated externalization. This is a call that has been presented by Negri and Hardt in their work on the reconstruction of the Common. They explain:

> It may well seem incongruous for us to celebrate entrepreneurship when neoliberal ideologues prattle on ceaselessly about its virtues, advocating the creation of an entrepreneurial society, bowing down in awe to the brave capitalist risk takers, and exhorting us all, from kindergarten to retirement, to become entrepreneurs of our own lives. We know such heroic tales of capitalist entrepreneurship are just empty talk, but if you look elsewhere you will see that there is plenty of entrepreneurial activity around today—organizing new social combinations, inventing new forms of social cooperation, generating democratic mechanisms for our access to, use of, and participation in decision-making about the common. It is important to claim the concept of entrepreneurship for our own.[45]

Using Negri and Hardt's thinking, self-provided housing can be understood as an entrepreneurial enterprise, but one that cuts links with a capitalist agenda. On the

contrary, such efforts suggest a reclamation of capital sovereignty over the infla-
tion and speculative nature of the housing market. The studies by architect Alastair
Parvin situate self-provisioning as a different value proposition for architects and
citizens. Parvin celebrates a "prosumer" culture, where consumers have become
producers of their own goods, not in the interest of corporations to cut costs by
externalizing labor, but rather in the capacity for self-empowerment and adaptation
to local contingencies. As he presents it:

> Although the basic stages of the project are unchanged, this creates a
> fundamentally different value-architecture. Most simply, because rather
> than designing for asset value generating shareholder profit, self-providers
> tend to design for long term use-value in the first place because they are
> the future users; designing a more generous house which is more appro-
> priate to their specific family needs (out of self-interest). Because of this,
> their houses are likely to be better in terms of energy performance and
> quality.[46]

Parvin relies on the capacity for self-provided labor from communities to propose
architectures that operate as a knowledge infrastructure; one that is formalized in a
construction system but also coexists as an Open-Source digital platform, allowing
the accumulation of knowledge to allow iteration and improvement of the design
alternatives over time. His project WikiHouse understands architecture as a multi-
layered cultural process where only a fraction is its formal manifestation. Parvin's
work builds upon a legacy of radical architects like Walter Segal, who understood
that for self-provisioning to be possible, architecture would need to develop methods, construction systems and models that would remove the friction and lower
the barrier of entry for citizens to participate in the value production of their
communities.

Architectural enclosures

This chapter has explored the pressures that neoliberal economics have placed over
the practice of architecture. Many of these pressures are presented in the form of
economic incentives that allow some key players to take advantage and display
power asymmetries over other members of the discipline. The practice of architecture today reflects a global condition of inequality, where a small number of
high-stakes commissions defines the aspiration of the field at large. Out of such
pressures, the Commons can be understood as social systems co-producing the
common goods that define a commonwealth for the discipline. Today, the Commons are under siege by market enclosures that seek to privatize and regulate access
to wealth produced socially. This battle is actively being fought through digital
networks, where large players have developed platforms for the extraction and gatekeeping of social wealth.

An Architecture for the Commons will need first to identify and separate itself
from its neoliberal counterpart, as the value systems that they utilize are at odds

with one another. We live in a time in history where the consolidation of oligopolies at different scales attempts to dictate and make a historic reading of the values and current tendencies. In architecture, the emergence of "Parametricism," as advocated by Patrik Schumacher, is the most prevalent reading of current market dynamics through the language of form and composition, understanding the discipline as a whole from its education, institutions and practice. In Schumacher's perspective, Parametricism constitutes an emergent epochal style of architecture, one that is founded on notions of liberal economics projecting a value proposition of freedom and order. Schumacher is a strong proponent of architecture's autonomy and the idea that the progress of a formal vocabulary should persist as a compass for the discipline.

There is a real danger for such claims to go unchallenged. Within the heuristics of Parametricism lie an attack on the potential of cooperative enterprises and collaborative production. Parametricism, as we will explore throughout the following chapter, has developed a vector of market enclosure, offering strategic advantages to larger industrial players. The emphasis on access, encapsulation of knowledge into design elements and cooperative digital platforms need to be disentangled from modes of production that are either co-opted by capital holders or plainly pursue vectors of progress that are detrimental to the prosperity of the city and its inhabitants. An Architecture for the Commons needs to be understood as an independent strand of architectural development, one that could coexist with its market counterpart. Its autonomy would only be possible through a participatory value system that might deviate from canonical trajectories.

Notes

1 Patrik Schumacher, 'The Progress of Geometry as Design Resource,' *Log*, 43 (2018), 1–15 <www.anycorp.com/>.
2 Schumacher, 'The Progress of Geometry as Design Resource.'
3 Patrik Schumacher, 'The Historical Pertinence of Parametricism and the Prospect of a Free Market Urban Order' in *The Politics of Parametricism: Digital Technologies in Architecture*, ed. by Mathew Poole and Manuel Shvartzberg (Bloomsbury Academic, 2015).
4 Kevin Kelly, *What Technology Wants* (Penguin Books, 2010).
5 Buckminster Fuller, *Nine Chains to the Moon* (Southern Illinois Univiversity Press, 1963).
6 Buckminster Fuller and Kiyoshi Kuromiya, *Critical Path* (St. Martin's Griffin, 1982).
7 Peter Joseph, *The New Human Rights Movement: Reinventing the Economy to End Oppression* (BenBella Books, 2017).
8 Jeremy Rifkin, *The Zero Marginal Cost Society* (Palgrave Macmillan, 2014).
9 Thomas Piketty, *Capital in the Twenty-First Century* (Belknap Press, An Imprint of Harvard University Press, 2014).
10 Pier Vittorio Aureli, *Less Is Enough: On Architecture and Asceticism* (Strelka Press, 2013).
11 Aureli, *Less Is Enough.*
12 Peggy Deamer, Quilian Riano, and Manuel Shvartzberg, 'Identifying the Designer as Worker', *MAS Context*, 27 (Fall 2015), 11.
13 Deamer, Riano, and Shvartzberg, 'Identifying the Designer as Worker', *MAS Context*, 27 (Fall 2015), 11.
14 The Architecture Lobby Inc, 'The Architecture Lobby', *MAS Context*, 27 (Fall 2015), 11.
15 Trebor Scholz, 'Digital Labor: New Opportunities, Old Inequalities,' *Re:Publica 2013*, 2013.

16 Scholz, 'Digital Labor.'
17 Shoshana Zuboff, *The Age of Surveillance Capitalism: The Fight for a Human Future at the New Frontier of Power* (PublicAffairs, 2019).
18 Mariana Mazzucato, *The Value of Everything: Making and Taking in the Global Economy* (PublicAffairs, 2018).
19 Zuboff, *The Age of Surveillance Capitalism.*
20 Mazzucato, *The Value of Everything.*
21 Joseph E. Stiglitz, *People, Power, and Profits: Progressive Capitalism for an Age of Discontent* (W. W. Norton & Company, 2019).
22 Stiglitz, *People, Power, and Profits.*
23 Garrett Hardin, 'The Tragedy of the Commons,' *Science*, 162.3859 (1968).
24 David Bollier, *Think Like a Commoner: A Short Introduction to the Life of the Commons* (New Society Publishers, 2014).
25 Elionor Ostrom, *Governing the Commons: The Evolution of Institutions for Collective Action* (Cambridge University Press, 2015).
26 Ostrom, *Governing the Commons.*
27 Massimo De Angelis, *Omnia Sunt Communia: On the Commons and the Transformation to Postcapitalism (In Common)* (Zed Books, 2017).
28 Bollier, *Think Like a Commoner.*
29 De Angelis, *Omnia Sunt Communia.*
30 Michael Hardt and Antonio Negri, *Assembly* (Oxford University Press, 2017).
31 Michael Hardt and Antonio Negri, *Multitude: War and Democracy in the Age of Empire* (Penguin Books, 2005).
32 De Angelis, *Omnia Sunt Communia.*
33 Tiziana Terranova, 'Debt and Autonomy: Lazzarato and the Constituent Powers of the Social,' 2013 http://thenewreader.org/Issues/1/DebtAndAutonomy.
34 Hardt and Negri, *Assembly.*
35 Reinier de Graaf, *Four Walls and a Roof* (Harvard University Press, 2017).
36 Christine Wall, 'Modular Men Architects, Labour and Standardisation in Mid-Twentieth-Century Britain,' in *Industries of Architecture (Critiques: Critical Studies in Architectural Humanities)* (Routledge, 2016).
37 Stavros Stavrides, *Common Space: The City as Commons (In Common)* (Zed Books, 2016).
38 Yochai Benkler, *The Wealth of Networks: How Social Production Transforms Markets and Freedom* (Yale University Press, 2006).
39 Tiziana Terranova, 'Capture All Work,' *Transmediale*, 2015.
40 Christian Marazzi, *The Violence of Financial Capitalism* (Semiotext(e), Los Angeles, 2011).
41 Marazzi, *The Violence of Financial Capitalism.*
42 Peggy Deamer, 'Architects, Really,' in *Can Architecture Be an Emancipatory Project? Dialogues on Architecture and the Left*, ed. by Nadir Z. Lahiji (Zero Books, 2016).
43 Aureli, *Less Is Enough.*
44 Ostrom, *Governing the Commons.*
45 Hardt and Negri, *Assembly.*
46 Alastair Parvin, David Saxby, Cristina Cerulli, and Tatjana Schneider. *A Right To Build* (Self-Published, London, 2011).

References

Aureli, Pier Vittorio, *Less Is Enough: On Architecture and Asceticism* (Strelka Press, Moscow, 2013)
Benkler, Yochai, *The Wealth of Networks: How Social Production Transforms Markets and Freedom* (Yale University Press, New Haven and New York, 2006)
Bollier, David, *Think Like a Commoner: A Short Introduction to the Life of the Commons* (New Society Publishers, Gabriola Island, 2014)

Deamer, Peggy, 'Architects, Really,' in *Can Architecture Be an Emancipatory Project? Dialogues on Architecture and the Left,* ed. by Nadir Z. Lahiji (Zero Books, Alresford, 2016)

De Angelis, Massimo, *Omnia Sunt Communia: On the Commons and the Transformation to Postcapitalism (In Common)* (Zed Books, London, 2017)

de Graaf, Reinier, *Four Walls and a Roof* (Harvard University Press, Cambridge, MA, and London, 2017)

Fuller, Buckminster, and Kuromiya, Kiyoshi, *Critical Path* (St. Martin's Griffin, New York, 1982)

Hardt, Michael, and Negri, Antonio, *Multitude: War and Democracy in the Age of Empire* (Penguin Books, New York, 2005)

———, *Assembly* (Oxford University Press, New York, 2017)

Joseph, Peter, *The New Human Rights Movement: Reinventing the Economy to End Oppression* (BenBella Books, Dallas, 2017)

Lanier, Jaron, *Who Own the Future* (Simon & Schuster, New York, 2013)

Marazzi, Christian, The Violence of Financial Capitalism (Semiotext(e), Los Angeles, 2011)

Ostrom, Elinor, *Governing the Commons: The Evolution of Institutions for Collective Action* (Cambridge University Press, Cambridge, 2015)

Parvin, Alastair, David Saxby, Cristina Cerulli, and Tatjana Schneider, *A Right to Build* (Self-Published, London, 2011)

Rifkin, Jeremy, The Zero Marginal Cost Society (Palgrave Macmillan, New York, 2014)

Scholz, Trebor, *Digital Labor: The Internet as Playground and Factory* (Routledge, New York, 2013)

Schumacher, Patrick, 'The Historical Pertinence of Parametricism and the Prospect of a Free Market Urban Order,' in *The Politics of Parametricism: Digital Technologies in Architecture*, ed. by Mathew Poole and Manuel Shvartzberg (Bloomsbury Academic, London and New York, 2015)

Srnicek, Nick, *Platform Capitalism* (Polity Press, Cambridge, 2017)

Stavrides, Stavros, *Common Space: The City as Commons (In Common)* (Zed Books, London, 2016)

Terranova, Tiziana, 'Debt and Autonomy: Lazzarato and the Constituent Powers of the Social,' 2013 <http://thenewreader.org/Issues/1/DebtAndAutonomy> [accessed 23 November 2017]

Wall, Christine, 'Modular Men Architects, Labour and Standardisation in Mid-Twentieth-Century Britain,' in *Industries of Architecture (Critiques: Critical Studies in Architectural Humanities)* (Routledge, New York, 2016)

2

THE COALESCENCE OF PARTS

Vertical integration

Through the study of the history of precision in manufacturing, author Simon Winchester explains the emergence of the paradigm of "interchangeable parts" throughout the 18th century, where identical parts could be exchanged if broken or malfunctioning.[1] This wasn't possible before reaching certain standards of precision that would allow the standardization of components. The first use of this principle, as Winchester points out, was in Paris in 1785, and it has become a foundation for modern industrial manufacturing until this day. For Winchester, the possibility to serially produce identical units allowed for a radical new form of efficiency, as generic precise parts would fit into a multiplicity of mechanical contexts, providing great flexibility for production. Moreover, it was the technical achievement of precision in "flatness" that triggered the opportunity for mechanical parts to engage in a geometrical dialogue of co-dependence with other parts that may come to be produced in the future, generating a standard for geometric cooperation.

Economist W. Brian Arthur has built upon the characteristics of mechanical devices to adventure a general definition of technology that relies on a nested relation of autonomous components that combined produce a functional assembly. For Arthur, technology is a combination of components, where each part has a form of encapsulated knowledge.[2] This definition of technology has a recursive function, as components in themselves can be a combination of components, allowing for the nesting of technologies within other technologies. This phenomenon can be observed in many devices, as functional objects can be disassembled into a series of autonomous and operational parts that can in themselves be disassembled into further functional units.

The principle of interchangeable parts and nested functionality are core pillars to today's manufacturing economy. Most manufacturing enterprises have developed business models to supply parts for multiple industries. It is rare that a company would internally manufacture all the parts necessary for the final product, as it will rely on the specialization of parts developed by external suppliers. But we have reached a state where it has become increasingly difficult to improve the performance of a product just by relying on generic components that are readily available.

Companies such as Tesla have disrupted the manufacturing ecosystem by adopting a form of radical "vertical integration." Vertical integration refers to the process where a company can stop relying on external suppliers by internalizing production. In the example of Tesla, the company has been able to develop 80% of its components in-house, greatly reducing the costs and improving the performance of the product. Elon Musk has used this same principle in SpaceX for the disruption of the space industry, where many suppliers would work as aggregators, each of them with their own gains, thereby increasing the cost of the final rocket. Musk has been celebrated for "cutting down the fat" of the manufacturing process and enabling more efficient assemblies.

Companies like Relativity, also operating in the space industry, have put forward products like the Aeon 1 engine, which is primarily manufactured through 3-D printing technology. The 3-D printing of the engine allows Relativity to cut the lead time in the production of the engine as well as radically reduce the number of parts that are necessary for its fabrication.[3]

Facing these recent technological developments, Arthur's definition[4] of nested components seems to play against the performance of a particular technology. It is

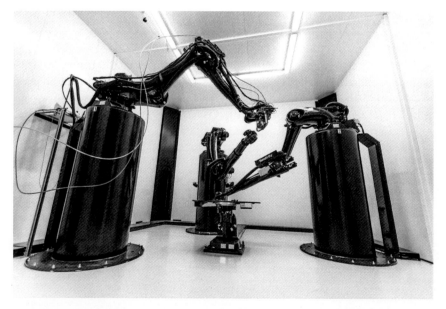

FIGURE 2.1 Relativity Space 3-D printing facility.

Source: Relativity Space

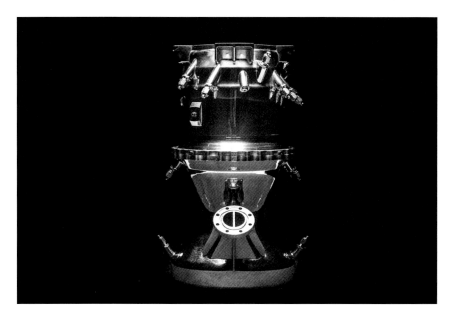

FIGURE 2.2   Aeon 1 Engine by Relativity Space. Engine is manufactured using 3-D printing technology, greatly reducing the number of parts.

Source: Relativity Space

possible that the most efficient technology would reduce the number of generic parts that could be used and trend toward the optimization of units without subparts, e.g., autonomous wholes that perform a unique narrow function. This is possible considering technologies like 3-D printing that would theoretically be able to manufacture specific units devoid of joinery or subcomponents.

What we can observe is that the increasing aspiration in efficiency and optimization has led to a process of vertical integration, only possible by large accumulations of capital that are able to enclose a production chain. Vertical integration, in turn, has an effect on the tectonics of objects, reducing the need for parts. Such dissolution of tectonics trends toward performative wholes that do not rely on a paradigm of nested or interchangeable parts but rather one of seamless wholes.

The rise of vertical integration in architecture

The process of vertical integration obtained through a pursuit of optimization has its own manifestation in the field of architecture. In the last few words of his book *Digital Architecture Beyond Computers*,[5] Roberto Bottazzi recalls Frederick Kiesler's lament regarding the need of seven different contractors to build one wall, due to its need for concrete structure, steel, brick, plaster, paint and wooden moldings. Kiesler gives evidence to the logistical complexities associated with the coordination of autonomous economic agents. Bottazzi echoes the pursuit of digital technologies for the last 30 years when he suggests that through a vision of synthesis afforded by digital workflows and a continuous notion of space, it will finally be possible to integrate architectural production in the hands of a single fabricator. His description aligns with one of the strands of computational thinking in architecture: the parametric agenda. The parametric agenda, as we will examine in the following paragraphs, has emerged from the capacity to synthesize data through the use of software, allowing mathematics and geometrical constructs to define the continuity of space between otherwise disparate materials. Bottazzi's description,[6] following the promises of the parametric agenda, implies a form of vertical integration in the field of architecture, advocating for single actors to acquire full control over a process that is otherwise in the hands of a diverse and competitive multi-actor economy. As demonstrated by Elon Musk's Tesla Gigafactory, the economic efficiencies of vertical integration are undeniable, but they come with socioeconomic implications such as increasing the barrier of entry for new members into the market.

The parametric playbook, as it has grown out of the computational research since the early 1990s, defines only a portion of the design strategies that can be pursued with computational techniques. The task of identifying different ideologies within computational design thinking has become a challenge due to designers such as Patrik Schumacher who have argued that "Parametricism," or most recently "Tectonism," define epochal styles that encompass all computational design in an attempt to unify the field and generate a movement that could be compared to modernism.[7] Schumacher's ideas have provoked a strong disenfranchisement from a younger generation of designers who, while using computational techniques, do not align with the ideologies of parametric design. By defining a boundary and ideologies behind the use of parametric tools, we will be able to understand the design strategies and tools that live outside the parametricist umbrella. The objective of this analysis is to push back from a mindless pursuit of technological progress that generates social division through the concentration of power to just a few actors generating an asymmetric playing field and income inequality. The following chapters will present an opposition to the trend of vertical integration and its architectural manifestation in parametric thinking, understanding that an efficient society controlled by only a few individuals erodes democracy and ultimately hinders meaningful innovation that seeks prosperity.

Mortar over brick

Brick and mortar construction embodies two very different construction ideologies. Bricks define the domain of parts, as they are discrete industrially produced elements that define an assembly of a larger whole. Bricks define a world that can be quantized into units, and that through the very geometry of the brick, is constrained by the possible arrangements of this prefabricated module. Mortar defines the domain of flow. Through its viscosity and malleability, mortar is able to adapt and change form and breach small gaps. Different mixtures of mortar allow the

FIGURE 2.3 Bricktopia by Map13 utilizing RhinoVault by Philippe Block. The project displays how the discrete brick units conform to the simulated vault configuration.

changing of its properties, gradually transitioning between viscosities and allowing the material to be adapted to different specific contexts.

Two mathematical paradigms are described by these two material assemblages: the discrete model and the continuous model. The discrete is characterized in mathematics as identified as whole numbers. The continuous model can be identified by real numbers, also understood by numbers with a decimal representation. The discrete model has been a conventional form of production, where the production of identical parts, such as bricks, provide greater efficiency in scale. This strategy was expanded to almost every building material, as the advent of industrialization further reduced costs of mass production. As a result, the bespoke or customized became a form of luxury living, in opposition to the serialized production seen as a "cookie cutter" solution.

As explained by Greg Lynn in *Animate Form*,[8] the continuous paradigm was the central paradigm for innovation in the 1990s. Space was no longer understood as a neutral container but rather populated with forces, or vectors, that are able to deform and contribute to the defining of a given form. Lynn utilized this to understand animation as a process in which form evolves through the influence of intrinsic and extrinsic forces. Traditional discrete, static objects are exchanged with a process that can yield multiple outcomes. Drawing from studies of natural systems that have embryogenesis, this novel process of defining form required a paradigm shift from a system of elements to one of flows, where intensities could transition into features, defining a continuous whole of gradually interpolated differentiation.

> For me, it is calculus that was the subject of the issue and it is the discovery and implementation of calculus by architects that continues to drive the field in terms of formal and constructed complexity. The loss of the module in favor of the infinitesimal component and the displacement of the fragmentary collage by the intensive whole are the legacy of the introduction of calculus.[9]

For Lynn, the introduction of calculus and infinitesimal mathematics was a way to develop a concept of space that includes time and duration. The adoption of software tools from the animation industry enabled architects to engage with time and force modelling, e.g., opportunities offered by the introduction of calculus.

Philosopher Manuel DeLanda, who strongly contributed to the adoption of a Deleuzian ontology in architecture, explains that matter can be understood through two different series of properties: extensive and intensive. Extensive properties are divisible attributes that can be notated in a Cartesian notion of space, like size, mass, area or volume. On the other hand, intensive properties are indivisible attributes that operate in a differential space, such as temperature, pressure or curvature. Intensities are considered prior to form, as they constitute attributes that can trigger form in the process of unfolding, which generates features.[10] Architecture that is defined by intensive properties was pioneered by Bernard Cache, who coined the term "objectile." This is an object that, framed in Deleuzian terms, is defined prior to its actualization, living in pure virtuality. As Cache explains,

> Objectile is a generic object: an open-ended algorithm, and a generative, incomplete notation, which becomes a specific object only when each parameter is assigned a value. In the same way, a parametric function notates a family of curves, but none in particular.[11]

Design could be conceived as an embryonic process out of which a multiplicity of variations could be obtained, each one of them different from the next. This development also allowed design to engage explicitly with the concept of the virtual. As Lynn explains, the virtual is understood as the abstract space of possible actualization.[12] The equations derived from calculus gave birth to parametric form, one in which populations of variables are able to define a solution space or domain of possible variations.

The shift toward intensive over extensive properties reached a culminating exposition in December 2003, when Frederic Migayrou curated the exhibition Architectures Non-Standard at Centre Pompidou, Paris, France. In the exhibition, the influence of the mathematics of calculus originated by Henri Poincaré established a direct relation with the spline architectures enabled by the software platforms available at the time.[13] Migayrou's exhibition gathered the work of Greg Lynn, Kas

Oosterhuis, Bernard Cache, UN Studio, Asymptote, dECOI, DR_D, Servo, R&Sie, Tom Kovac, Kol/MAC Studio and NOX. While all these architects had developed specific design research through the advancement of digital technologies, many of the core principles, such as mass customization through parametric differentiation, performative geometries or file-to-factory protocols have transferred and become standard practice for architectural firms worldwide.

The design research in nonstandard architecture that was developed throughout the 1990s led to a set of practices that constituted a design paradigm of continuity. Developments in digital fabrication linked to this paradigm started to enable the post-rationalization and fabrication of complex geometries that emerged from animation software. Digital fabrication allowed the serialization of identical parts to be considered an issue of the past, as it allows for bespoke form to be as viable economically as its serialized counterpart. As it has been framed by Mario Carpo, nonstandard seriality made economies of scale irrelevant, as digital production could, at least in theory, allow for the fabrication of unique components with no additional cost.[14] The rationale behind this statement came from examples such as the CNC milling machine, which could produce bespoke units in the same time that would produce identical ones. According to Carpo:

> In a digital production process, standardization is no longer a money-saver. Likewise, customization is no longer a money-waster.[15]

The file-to-factory protocol allowed digital models to directly provide instructions for CNC manufacturing, circumventing the need for traditional architectural representation outside of the computer screen. The digital model became an apparatus for gathering architectural data and a protocol for collaboration and coordination. Moreover, the multiplicity embedded in the parametric variation of a digital model no longer describes one building but families of buildings. Software companies, together with a new generation of architects and tool makers, developed the digital infrastructure that has enabled the adoption of these tools by students as well as industry. Over time, the terminology describing this area of work became "parametric design."

Parametric design

The term "parametric design" describes how a given parameter—or data—is able to determine a specific outcome out of the multiplicity provided by a domain. An example of a parameter could be the floor to ceiling height in a tower project. Such parameter could define the overall subdivision of the building mass and generate variation in the final number of floors. Through the use of computer programming or scripting, architects started to engage with procedural definitions, e.g., sequential rulesets that could cascade into one another, determined by the specified parameters. The mathematical and logical relationships that form became the basis of associative geometries that would further characterize the evolution of parametric principles.

Parametric design is characterized by tools of interpolation. The gradient becomes a design tool allowing transitions between a multiplicity of design constraints. This is the way in which spline modeling started to impact the world of designers, offering geometric construct with a small number of control points that would result in a mathematically interpolated curve. Spline modeling can be found to be the basis of many software algorithms and tools used to facilitate design. For example, the Catmull–Clark algorithm integrated into Autodesk Maya software allows the transition from polygonal geometries to intensive plastic topologies. Marching Cubes algorithms allow the generation of geometries and surfaces using any number of isolated inputs, merging discreteness into unified shells. Software

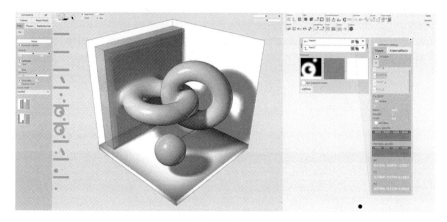

FIGURE 2.4   Monolith Interface for voxel-based modeling developed by Andrew Payne.

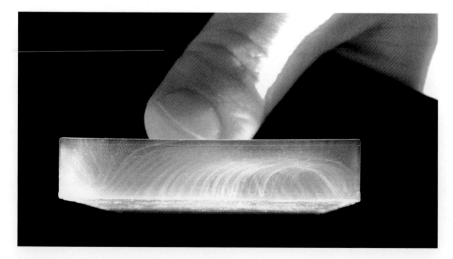

FIGURE 2.5   Graded 3-D printed material intensities produced with Monolith developed by Panagiotis Michalatos.

such as Monolith, developed by Payne and Michalatos,[16] provides the infrastructure to think of form as a pixel field of materials—a voxel—that can gradually transition between properties of color, elasticity and opacity, linking directly with the most advanced 3-D printing technologies currently available. The Grasshopper plug-in for Rhino[17] constitutes one of the most widely adopted pieces of digital infrastructure for the development of the continuous paradigm, allowing its users to parametrize all the possible variables in a piece of geometry.

A parametric definition can be characterized by the "slider"; a digital construct within the parametric repertoire that allows designers to suspend the necessity

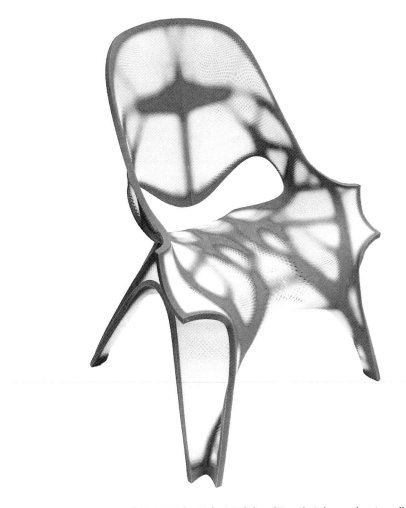

FIGURE 2.6   3-D printed CHAIR by Zaha Hadid and Patrik Schumacher in collaboration with STRATASYS, 3-D printed on the Stratasys Objet1000 Multi-Material 3-D Printer.

Source: Courtesy of Zaha Hadid Architects

FIGURE 2.7   The Heydar Aliyev Center in Baku by Zaha Hadid Architects. The design demonstrates Schumacher's view of parametric articulation, interpolating the building with the landscape. The project portrays the dissolution of tectonics, where details are minimized in favor of the fluidity of form.

Source: Courtesy of Zaha Hadid Architects

for decision making, allowing decisions to become a variable that exists within a domain. As the slider starts to recur through a parametric model, the model grows in its multiplicity of possible outcomes, defining not a particular solution but a solution space. This solution space defines final form through a complex interplay with clients, budgets and regulations.

The commercial adoption of parametric strategies is linked to the ability to digitally simulate large populations of possible designs and testing them with performative criteria. The testing of different parameters, using sliders positioned against a given performative criteria such as structural efficiency, mean that some solutions perform better than others. This process, known as optimization, has been widely adopted by large architecture and engineering practices in the past decades.

Architects such as Kostas Terzidis have claimed that in the model of parametric optimization, design becomes a permutation enterprise, where the search for the optimal parameters for a given design problem can yield an objectively better solution.[18] Such assessment requires us to first accept that there could be an optimal solution to the problem of architecture. The strategy of parametric design could be then understood as practice of model making that declares the boundaries of a problem, variables to be considered and by omission, variables to be excluded. The definition of such a mathematical domain also assumes that an answer to a design problem lives within the domain specified, validating the tools that have been generated for its resolution. The notion of optimization has its own tradition in architecture modeling, as it pre-dates digital technologies. As we will evaluate later, architect-engineer Frei Otto since the 1960s developed a framework for modeling form founded in the notion of optimization and self-organization he called "form finding."

Form finding—design as search

Frei Otto understood that form wasn't a neutral container. Through complex material experiments at the Institute of Lightweight Structures in Stuttgart, Otto was able to allow for the "self-organization" of form in design. This is a technique that had been pioneered by Antonio Gaudi in the physical calculation of the vaulting of the Sagrada Familia in Barcelona in the late 19th and early 20th centuries. From hundreds of experiments Otto was able to derive optimal form by allowing the forces of stress to reach a state of equilibrium. He demonstrated these principles through the use of soap bubbles, where surface tension forces the thin membrane of the bubbles to conform into spherical arrangements. When introducing external elements, soap bubbles would self-organize to determine an optimal solution to the problem of force. The emergent minimal surface is a physical phenomenon obtained by the optimization of stress under interpolation constrains.

Form finding suggests that the act of designing becomes a search for an optimal solution. Adopted from evolutionary biology, the notion of the fittest design is considered validation criteria for an architecture that has been conceived as a puzzle, where one solution presents the ideal response to a problem of performance. The practice of material computation, from a parametric perspective, inherently declares the variables associated with structural stability as the key field to be evaluated and changed to reach to an optimal structure. It hasn't been until the advent of digital simulations, with techniques such as spring-relaxation or subdivision algorithms, that the practice of form finding could include architectural variables beyond structure, such as inhabitation areas, light exposure, egress paths, etc. These are criteria that experiments in material computation would have missed, as physical materials are agnostic to the series of overlapping objectives of an architectural agenda. In physical form finding, the hierarchical imperative is gravity and self-support, digital form finding allowed the negotiation of material parameters with a larger pool of architectural concerns. What emerges out of the accumulation of design parameters in a model is that inevitably, there will be criteria that counteract one another at the moment of evaluating one form of performance; for instance, as exemplified by John Frazer in one of his lectures in 2014,[19] the width of the hull of a vessel will affect its speed and its potential inhabitation at opposite ends of the variable's domain. In such a case, the designer cannot just rely on form finding but must first decide what criteria is most relevant for the brief in hand. Or, as has been presented by philosopher and Professor Steven Shaviro as an argument against methodologies of self-organization:

> No self-organizing system can obviate the need for such a decision, or dictate what it will be. And decision always implies novelty or difference—in this way it is absolutely incompatible with notions of autopoiesis, homeostasis, or Spinoza's conatus. What we need is an aesthetics of decision, instead of our current metaphysics of emergence.[20]

While suppressing concerns like budget or ethical labor practices can yield exuberance, form is always an act of decision making. Design is the selection of a series of parameters and criteria over others. A naïve form of computation suggests that there is indeed an optimal form, one that might be able to consider all the available parameters and objectively determine the apex of a fitness landscape, but as some criteria are privileged, others will inevitably be disregarded. This form of optimization demarcates a boundary between the object and the environment, implying that the optimization can only be operated over the object of governance. The object becomes an island, able to optimize all its internal components but speciates from any further couplings.

If we focus our attention at the fitness landscape, and observe design as a probabilistic event defined by all the degrees of freedom enabled by a parametric equation, we can identify that such landscape does not offer all real design solutions. Such a fitness landscape needs to be understood as a system of expectations.

Expectations in the fitness landscape

Lebanese-American scholar Nassim Taleb has developed the concept of a Black Swan to describe events that lie outside the realm of regular expectations. For Taleb, these events are disruptive, as they could not have been predicted prior to their occurrence. He presents such events as outliers. Only after their unexpected occurrence are we able to post-rationalize and define a new system of expectations that includes them. When describing a Black Swan event, Taleb writes;

> First, it is an outlier, as it lies outside the realm of regular expectations, because nothing in the past can convincingly point to its possibility. Second, it carries an extreme impact. Third, in spite of its outlier status, human nature makes us concoct explanations for its occurrence after the fact, making it explainable and predictable.[21]

Building upon Taleb's ideas, philosopher Elie Ayache has further developed three different understandings of the Black Swan concept defined by Taleb. As he explains:

> Of the three different sources of Black Swans that Taleb describes in his book: (1) the Black Swan that is inherent in our genes and in our evolutionary blindness to extreme events (I have always disliked naturalized epistemology), (2) the Black Swan, or rather the Gray Swan, that is the result of mistaking the Gaussian probability distribution of Mediocristan for what should be, "in reality," the scalable laws of Extremistan (I will come to that below) and (3) the Black Swan that cannot possibly be predicted because it falls beyond knowledge and probability (that is to say, it falls beyond the given range of possibility), I retain the third as the philosophical one (therefore worthy of my attention). The other two are either merely anthropological or disappointingly metaphysical.[22]

From a parametric perspective, design could be understood as a Black Swan event that exists within a fitness landscape. The parametric interpretation of form finding follows Ayache's first model: an optimistic expectation that a Black Swan (equated to an optimal design) is a highly improbable combination of parameters yet perfectly possible within the fitness landscape. Design, from this perspective, could be seen as a search protocol that seeks for performative data configurations within a large universe of possibilities. The ability to intuitively navigate such a landscape is regarded as talent in designers, but this also opens the door for algorithmic processes such as artificial intelligence which in recent years has become increasingly good at mimicking humans at the moment of selecting data patterns.

Ayache's third approach offers a radically different model: he suggests that a Black Swan lives in a completely different plane, one oblique to the system of expectations defined in the possibility space parameters.[23] This model suggest that a parametric model should always be considered potentially incomplete, unable to register the true domain of the problem. Taking this idea further, it is possible to understand these parametric models as a form of rhetoric that persuasively defines a domain as a justification of outcomes. The problem of the Black Swan in design offers a window into the value proposition of architects, where the rhetoric of a vast (yet incomplete) possibility space is systematically explored in order to find heroic outliers. The brilliance of the parametric model, as a rhetoric device, has been the construction of a possibility space constituted by 99% of virtual waste that only serves as an alibi for final proposals.

A productive understanding of the notion of Black Swans in design relies on understanding inherited blind spots in our system of expectations and advocates for reinvigorating our skepticism over rhetorical models such as parametric optimization. For Ayache, the third form of Black Swan he describes should follow a different name; he calls it a "Blank Swan." As he explains:

> The Black Swan is the perfectly unexpected event; the White Swan is the perfectly expected event. Underlying both is the category of prediction and prevision, which is the real object of my criticism. The Black Swan refers to something we cannot see or foresee (it is black) and the White Swan to something evident and clear. Although opposed, the two are predicated on the idea of content of vision, or content of mind, or content of expectation.
>
> What if we completely eliminated the content of vision, i.e. both the colours White and Black? What if we eliminated the whole context of colour and of content? Hence the BLANK Swan.[24]

For Ayache, the Black Swan is an outlier but still bound to the solution space; the Blank Swan, on the other hand, defies such a system altogether. It is possible to interpret this as just some missing parameter in a parametric model; the unexpected event provides an update of new variables that need to be considered in order to develop a prediction. This misses the point. Ayache develops the notion of contingent claims to argue for events that acquire meaning and value only once they are written or committed into operation. This means that no post-rationalization of the Blank Swan will be able to conform it back to the parametrized solution space and conform it to a fitness landscape. Ayache argues that events such as writing or the process of pricing the market are events that do not emerge from a probability.[25] This also applies to architectural design, and particularly to a critical analysis of how computational tools embed an attempt to anticipate and deny the expression of contingent cultural values.

Optimization as part-reduction

The technique of form finding, from a purely structural perspective, often results in curvilinear forms that negotiate the structural forces between established constraints. In order to fabricate these geometries, the use of programming has been incredibly useful, as an algorithm is able to subdivide and panelize highly intricate surfaces. Traditionally, in a mechanical paradigm, parts are manufactured following principles of standardization and arranged into larger assemblies. A series of parts would achieve a meaning or purpose, like executing an action, as in the case of a motor, giving rise to a "whole" that is more than the sum of its parts. The continuous paradigm understood that nature doesn't operate with these mechanical principles, as nature is able to gradually differentiate intensities at a microscopic level, allowing parts to operate fluidly within a field. The mechanical paradigm, therefore, has been challenged by a new organicist paradigm that would "grow"[26] form as opposed to assembling it.

Strategies of part reduction through coalescence proposes dissolution of tectonics, allowing smaller microscopic units like fibers (as in the case of composites) or fully fluid materialities (as is the case with contour crafting) to define architectural morphology. This would enable the materialization of the fluid curvilinear shapes emerging from parametric design software, defining a taxonomy of novel tectonics.[27] Following the continuous model, assemblies of discrete parts are slowly replaced by smaller and smaller elements such as filaments and fibers that are able to coalesce into larger shells not through mechanical connections but chemical ones. Tectonics is placed in opposition to composites, where accumulation and phase-changing properties are able to derive shells from gradient arrangements. As presented by Greg Lynn:

> The term tectonic is a term that architects love to use as it reminds them of their affection for large collections of mechanically assembled parts. Architecture, probably more than most fields, deals with a great number of parts, their management, their assembly and most importantly, their expression as discrete parts. It's inevitable that we are going to have to deal with tectonics; however, the more I know about composites the more I hate things like screws, nails, bolts, and everything else associated with mechanical rather than chemical connections. It's incredible how annoyed I get when I see twenty thousand dollars of stainless bolts weighing several thousand pounds arrive at a job site. I'd rather have glue; I'm a big, big glue fan.[28]

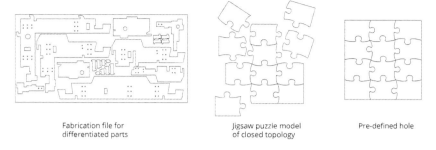

Fabrication file for
differentiated parts

Jigsaw puzzle model
of closed topology

Pre-defined hole

FIGURE 2.8 Diagram of the jigsaw puzzle analogy referring to the result of post rationalizing geometry for CNC milling fabrication.

The espousal of chemical connections over mechanical ones points to a hierarchy of the continuous over the discrete, where parts are subservient to a whole, fulfilling a unique role in a larger assembly just like in the jigsaw puzzle.

The process of modeling and fabricating under the continuous paradigm has been described by Patrik Schumacher[29] as parametric articulation, placing emphasis on the fact that such techniques leave behind the toolbox of composition as a form generator, the legacy of the modern and postmodern movement which relied on the arrangement of discrete units in space. The term "articulation," in the eyes of Schumacher, describes the intensive dynamic process of negotiation between forces that ultimately arrive to smooth forms that synthesize the series of variables that are used as inputs.

An optimization technique that makes evident the parametric coalescence of parts is the algorithm of topological optimization; where inputs are placed within a voxelized container represented as a solid mass, and an iterative process is gradually able to remove the mass that does not perform structural load. In order to achieve this, the algorithm simulates the lines of stress, tension and compression that the mass would have to resist based on the constraints established as inputs. This algorithm has been used as a flagship demonstration by companies such as Autodesk of how computational design could generate unexpected solutions that have been optimized for material and manufacturing performance. One of the key capabilities of topological optimization is to override the need of mechanical subcomponents, as it is able to look at the internal forces within a digital model and come up with a singular new topology that performs what previously had been done by several interdependent parts. The algorithm is informed with the capabilities of additive manufacturing, allowing the generation of unique new topologies that reduce the need for parts and material. As discussed previously with the case of the Aeon Engine, here part reduction is a key factor for the optimization of form. This is what the industry calls "disruptive"; an economic opportunity to bypass an established production chain, internalizing the production of a building element through new manufacturing methods. Optimization through part reduction aims to attack not only the inefficiencies in structural performance but more importantly, the inefficiencies and redundancies in a production chain. This optimization perspective idealizes a fully integrated production chain that is able to correct and improve efficiency (and profitability) of any building system.

Here it becomes clear how the foundations and ideologies of parametric design as a framework for optimization can generate a trend toward vertical integration. This trend is founded in the alignment between the articulation of form using

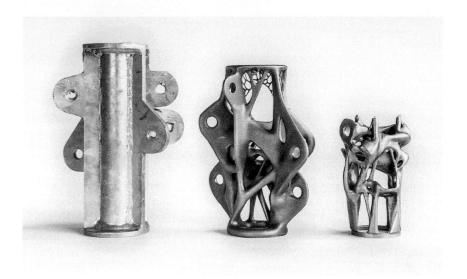

FIGURE 2.9 Topological Optimization technique used for the design of a metallic joint manufactured through 3-D printing technology.

Source: Project by Arup. © Davidfotografie.

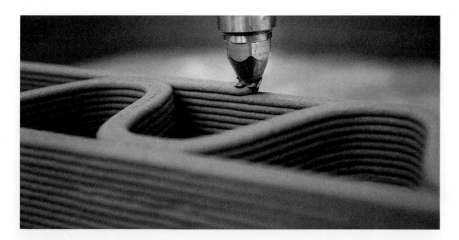

FIGURE 2.10 Contour Crafting manufacturing. Extruder is able to print layers of viscous material such as concrete.

Source: Image courtesy of XtreeE.

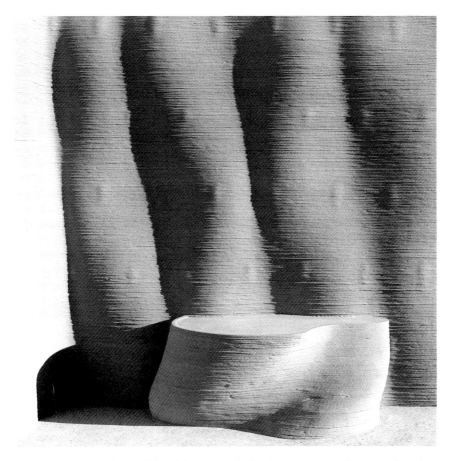

FIGURE 2.11   USH Sinusoidal Wall by XtreeE built using contour crafting manufacturing.

Source: Image courtesy of XtreeE.

continuous methodologies and the capitalist imperative for increasing performance. As discussed in Chapter 1, the progressive ephemeralization of building technologies can effectively produce lighter and cheaper buildings, but under a fully integrated framework only those sitting at the top of such enterprise are able to reap the benefits of their production.

The swarm fallacy

Since the release of *The Autopoiesis of Architecture*,[30] Patrik Schumacher has advocated elevating the use of parametric design techniques to the status of an architectural style he calls "Parametricism." For Schumacher, parametric design is a strategy not only to address the issue of design and form but also to open up links that the discipline shares with our current economic system, forms of practice and education, as well as the societal organization through the design of large-scale projects and cities. At the core of his vision is the idea or articulation or mediation between stakeholders. The curvilinearity of design is suggested to be the result of a difficult equation between a myriad of parameters. The heuristics of Parametricism as Schumacher defined it in 2011 included functional heuristics such as avoiding functional stereotypes and formal heuristics such as smooth differentiation,[31] The formal heuristics of Schumacher overlaps with the continuous paradigm we have discussed in this chapter, as he recognizes the foundational impact that non-standard calculus offered for the discipline. Like Lynn, he also understood space as a dynamic medium. As Schumacher explains, "modernism was founded on the concept of space. Parametricism differentiates fields. Fields are full, as if filled with a fluid medium."[32] While the advocacy for formal heuristics appears innocent, Schumacher quickly establishes a link between curvilinearity and articulation as an organizational strategy representative of free-market economics. He rejects top-down interventions in the urban fabric and suggests that the market operates as a self-organizing bottom-up process, one in which "only market processes can process the new diversity and complexity of information, and generate the knowledge required to deliver land and real state resources reliably to productive and desired uses, avoiding wasteful misallocation."[33] Schumacher seems to contradict himself as he has also gone on record to discuss how market economics often generate "garbage spill" urbanism,[34] and that Parametricism is able to provide a legible spatial order without becoming a top-down strategy. As Schumacher writes,

> While laissez-faire development can deliver a socially (market) validated program mix and program distribution, it seems bound to produce a visual chaos in the urban dimension. The visual disorder in not only ugly and distracting; it is disorienting, and thus compromises the societal functionality of the built environment. The articulation of a legible social order—the architect's core competency—is itself a vital aspect not only of the city's 'livability' but also of its economic productivity.[35]

Therefore, Parametricism attempts to position itself against the rigid imposition of form, and against the laissez-faire development that ultimately contributes, in the view of Schumacher, to urban chaos. Parametricism attempts to present itself as a malleable design response to markets founded on ideas borrowed from the natural sciences in the study of complex adaptive systems and emergent phenomena. Utilizing agent-based modeling techniques, or algorithmic swarms, Parametricism can claim to develop bottom-up design, which, like the market, can self-organize and adapt a multiplicity of input variables and represent different stakeholders. However, swarm strategies are also able to obfuscate decision making. As many other forms of artificial intelligence, algorithmic swarms acquire autonomy and agency, dictated by the objectives of its programming author. What these techniques truly obfuscate is that the implementation of algorithmic swarms always relies on a top-down choreographer, a decision-making process that defines what is included and excluded from a model and what are the strengths or weights used by each agent to influence the general system.

While branded on the rhetoric of emergence, Parametricism is truly able to exercise top-down design, enabled by the obfuscation behind black-box algorithms.

Parametricism utilizes complexity theory and emergence to provide validation through a form of natural order. The image of the swarm is cast as a visual diagram of Schumacher's claim when he states "*Parametricism*. Its most conspicuous outward characteristic is a complex and dynamic curvilinearity accentuated by a swarm-like proliferation of continuously differentiated components."[36] While algorithmic simulated swarms are an effective means to study and understand self-organization and systems design, there is a danger of extrapolating the inherit self-organizing properties of such closed systems to the qualities of architecture or cities. From a technical standpoint, the use of swarm algorithms for architectural design are not engaging with the phenomenon of self-organization as observed in the natural world and culture, as the digital models operate within constrained parametric domain—therefore defining a closed system.

Agent-based modeling is argued as a non-deterministic system, and this is true when dealing with unexpected or even minuscule deviations in data that can affect a simulation, generating a non-repeatable solution each time the algorithm is calculated. However, this is not the case in a form of agent-based simulation often used by parametric designers where the digital environment in which the algorithms are executed internally defines all variables, as such a closed system effectively becomes a deterministic technique. The fact that these algorithms are presented as operating over a time-lapse is irrelevant to defining them as non-deterministic. The variable of time becomes a parametric slider that can be moved back and forth and will arrive at the exact same solution each time. These issues point out incoherencies in Parametricism, revealing a strategy of obfuscation where disciplinary research genuinely interested in self-organization and open-ended systems, is co-opted by the argument for a formal style that is rigid and authoritative. The brand of aesthetics emerging from "nature's complexity" remains top-down.

Architecture critic Manuel Shvartzberg develops an excellent historical recollection of the development of swarm algorithms, from the work of Craig Reynolds to the development of the Logo platform by Seymour Papert.[37] While Shvartzberg sees swarms as a form of techno-cultural infrastructure that has contributed to the development of the individual as a self-directed agent who has acquired the "pleasure of commanding," this judgment falls into the assumption that parametric design is indeed the result of self-organizing ideology in maturation for several decades. Shvartzberg states that an example of the appropriation of the swarm for use in the architectural vocabulary can be seen in the "parametric urbanism" exercises of Zaha Hadid Architects, as used in the cover of *The Politics of Parametrics*,[38] where the image of the swarm is clearly identifiable. However, this is the swarm fallacy, deterministic architecture models constrained to a parametric domain argued for as open and adaptable. The ability to develop "swarm-like" or "swarm-looking" urbanism needs to be assessed as part of the rhetoric of bio-validation exercised by the parametric agenda.

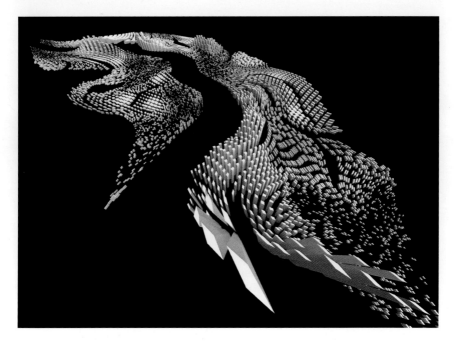

FIGURE 2.12 Thames Gateway as an urban field courtesy Zaha Hadid Architects. The image was used in the cover of *The Politics of Parametricism* by Matthew Poole and Manuel Shvartzberg in reference to swarm systems.

Source: Courtesy of Zaha Hadid Architects

Fully integrated Parametricism

Beyond the academic discourse developed around parametric techniques, the economic efficiencies of the model have been picked up by the building industry for the development of competitive models for construction. The trend toward vertical integration afforded by the parametric model is accentuated by an economic period where large concentrations of capital are at the disposal of a small number of individuals capable of "disrupting" distributed production through internalization. The narrative of Parametricism makes no intentional attempt to monopolize the market or increase the barrier of entry to architectural production through practices of vertical integration, so we could assume that these consequences are unintended but welcomed, offering a strategic advantage over competitors. While the attempts to develop a parametric urbanism have gone largely unfulfilled, the true face of Parametricism that comes with a clear economic understanding of the need for fully vertically integrated production chains, can be observed in companies such as Katerra. Katerra, a company that has been funded by capital developed in the technology sector, aims to disrupt architectural production focusing on the optimization of building elements using parametric techniques and implementing a vertically integrated production chain. Katerra, following the model of companies such as Apple, have started pitching for their architecture solutions, demonstrating how their product offers undeniable economic improvements to the market. In this context is where parametric techniques, optimization and vertical integration really shine, offering a predictable value proposition for predefined typology of architecture.

As presented by Taylor Keep, head of building science at Katerra, during the "Prototyping Collective Space" symposium,[39] competitors will really struggle to keep up with Katerra, suggesting that the efficiencies achieved by the company through vertical integration would require new participants to the industry to make an initial investment of at least $250 million to compete. Vertical integration can lead to vertical monopolies, increasing the barrier of entry and generating a process of "speciation," where new potentially copyrighted solutions are no longer compatible with other parts in the market, attempting to generate closed design ecosystems. Vertical integration has a profound impact on tectonics, allowing for new optimized copyrighted parts emerging out of the coalescence of generic components. This process gives immense protections to manufacturers not only in production but also throughout the lifespan of objects. Companies are able to introduce proprietary parts that will force users to seek affiliated repair services in case of a malfunction. As has been pointed out by the "Right to Repair" movement, a critical example occurred in 2009 when Apple introduced the pentalobe screw, designed to alienate users from opening devices and forcing them to seek repairs within the Apple ecosystem. This has given the opportunity for Apple, as has been reported by thousands of customers, to inflate the cost of repairs, which incentivizes the purchase of new items.

The economic danger of vertical integration is the reduction of market diversity, which ensures the perpetuation of the success of already established practices. At a deeper level, the optimization protocol at the core of the fully integrated parametric

FIGURE 2.13   Detail of iPhone utilizing the Pentalobe Screws designed by Apple.

network, operating under market incentives, impedes any form of architectural open-endedness. The mapping, acquisition and "disruption" of a production chains formalizes a centralized notion of control far from the rhetoric of emergence and adaptability. Parametricism in this sense attempts, through a narrative of simulation and design articulation, to elevate the decision making of architects and designers with the capacity to dictate what is valuable and what is not. This implies the erroneous and dangerous assumption that a simulation model can indeed demarcate what should be included as an architectural variable. This foreshadows the collapse of forms of architecture that are diverse, idiosyncratic and capable of defining their own value system.

Notes

1 Simon Winchester, *The Perfectionists: How Precision Engineers Created the Modern World* (Harper, 2018).
2 William Brian Arthur, *The Nature of Technology: What It Is and How It Evolves* (Free Press, 2009).
3 'Relativity Space' <www.relativityspace.com/aeon>.
4 Arthur.
5 Roberto Bottazzi, *Digital Architecture Beyond Computers: Fragments of a Cultural History of Computational Design* (Bloomsbury Visual Arts, 2018).
6 Bottazzi, *Digital Architecture Beyond Computers.*
7 Patrik Schumacher, *The Autopoiesis of Architecture: A New Framework for Architecture* (Wiley, 2011).
8 Greg Lynn, *Animate Form* (Princeton Architectural Press, 1999).
9 Greg Lynn, 'Folding in Architecture,' *AD* March–April (Wiley, Chichester, 1993).
10 Manuel Delanda, *Intensive Science Virtual Philosophy* (Continuum International Publishing Group, 2006).
11 Bernard Cache, *Projectiles* (Architectural Association Publications, 2011).
12 Lynn, *Animate Form.*
13 Frédéric Migayrou, *Architectures Non Standard*, Centre Georges Pompidou Service Commercial (Centre Georges Pompidou Service Commercial, 2004). Edited by Éditions du Centre Pompidou, Paris, 2003. [accessed 13 April 2014].
14 Mario Carpo, *The Alphabet and the Algorithm* (MIT Press, 2011).
15 Carpo, *The Alphabet and the Algorithm.*
16 Michalatos Panagiotis and Andrew Payne, 'Monolith : The Biomedical Paradigm and the Inner Complexity of Hierarchical Material Design,' *Complexity & Simplicity–Proceedings of the 34th ECAADe Conference*, 1 (2016), 445–454.
17 David Rutten, 'Grasshopper Interface Explained,' 2015 <https://wiki.mcneel.com/labs/explicithistory/interfaceexplained>. [accessed 6 June 2018].
18 Kostas Terzidis, *Permutation Design: Buildings, Texts, and Contexts* (Routledge, 2015).
19 John Frazer, 'Computational Design,' 2014 <https://egs.edu/faculty/john-frazer/lectures>.
20 Steven Shaviro, 'Against Self-Organization,' *The Pinocchio Theory* (2009). Blog post <http://www.shaviro.com/Blog/?p=756> [accessed September 2013].
21 Nassim Nicholas Taleb, *The Black Swan: The Impact of the Highly Improbable* (Random House, 2007).
22 Elie Ayache, *The Blank Swan: The End of Probability* (Wiley, 2010).
23 Ayache, *The Blank Swan.*
24 Ayache, *The Blank Swan.*
25 Ayache, *The Blank Swan.*
26 Neri Oxman, 'Structuring Design Fabrication of Heterogeneous,' *Applied Physics Letters*, 80.4 (2010), 78–85.

27 Jesse Reiser and Nanako Umemoto, *Atlas of Novel Tectonics* (Princeton Architectural Press, 2006).

28 Greg Lynn and Mark Foster Gage, *Composites, Surfaces, and Software: High Performance Architecture* (Yale School of Architecture, 2011).

29 Patrik Schumacher, *The Autopoiesis of Architecture, Volume II: A New Agenda for Architecture* (Wiley, 2012).

30 Schumacher, *The Autopoiesis of Architecture: A New Framework for Architecture.*

31 Schumacher, *The Autopoiesis of Architecture: A New Framework for Architecture.*

32 Schumacher, *The Autopoiesis of Architecture: A New Framework for Architecture.*

33 Schumacher, *The Autopoiesis of Architecture: A New Framework for Architecture.*

34 Patrik Schumacher, 'The Historical Pertinence of Parametricism and the Prospect of a Free Market Urban Order,' in *The Politics of Parametricism: Digital Technologies in Architecture,* ed. by Mathew Poole and Manuel Shvartzberg (Bloomsbury Academic, 2015).

35 Schumacher, 'The Historical Pertinence of Parametricism and the Prospect of a Free Market Urban Order.'

36 Schumacher, *The Autopoiesis of Architecture, Volume II: A New Agenda for Architecture.*

37 Mathew Poole and Manuel Shvartzberg, *The Politics of Parametricism: Digital Technologies in Architecture* (Bloomsbury Academic, 2015).

38 Poole and Shvartzberg, *The Politics of Parametricism.*

39 Taylor Keep, 'Better, Cheaper and Faster Buildings' [speech], *Prototyping Collective Space* (2019).

References

Arthur, William Brian, *The Nature of Technology: What It Is and How It Evolves* (Free Press, New York, 2009)

Ayache, Elie, *The Blank Swan: The End of Probability* (Wiley, Chichester, 2010)

Bottazzi, Roberto, *Digital Architecture Beyond Computers: Fragments of a Cultural History of Computational Design* (Bloomsbury Visual Arts, London, 2018)

Cache, Bernard, *Projectiles* (Architectural Association Publications, London, 2011)

Carpo, Mario, *The Alphabet and the Algorithm* (Massachusetts Institute of Technology Press, Cambridge, 2011)

DeLanda, Manuel, *Intensive Science Virtual Philosophy* (Continuum International Publishing Group, London and New York, 2006)

Frazer, John, 'Computational Design,' 2014 <https://egs.edu/faculty/john-frazer/lectures> [accessed 12 November 2018]

Keep, Taylor, 'Better, Cheaper and Faster Buildings' [speech], *Prototyping Collective Space* (2019)

Lynn, Greg, *Animate Form* (Princeton Architectural Press, New York, 1999)

———, Introduction of 'Folding in Architecture,' *Architectural Design*, March–April (Wiley, Chichester, 1993)

Lynn, Greg, and Mark Foster Gage, *Composites, Surfaces, and Software: High Performance Architecture* (Yale School of Architecture, New Haven, 2011)

Michalatos, Panagiotis, and Andrew Payne, 'Monolith: The Biomedical Paradigm and the Inner Complexity of Hierarchical Material Design,' *Complexity & Simplicity–Proceedings of the 34th ECAADe Conference*, 1 (2016), 445–454

Migayrou, Frédéric, *Architectures Non Standard*, *Centre Georges Pompidou Service Commercial* (Centre Georges Pompidou Service Commercial, 2004). Edited by Éditions du Centre Pompidou, Paris, 2003

Oxman, Neri, 'Structuring Design Fabrication of Heterogeneous,' *Architectural Design,* 80 (4), 78–85 (Wiley, Chichester, 2010)

Poole, Mathew, and Manuel Shvartzberg, *The Politics of Parametricism: Digital Technologies in Architecture* (Bloomsbury Academic, London, New York, 2015)

Reiser, Jesse, and Nanako Umemoto, *Atlas of Novel Tectonics* (Princeton Architectural Press, New York, 2006)

'Relativity Space' <www.relativityspace.com/aeon> [accessed 17 July 2019]

Rutten, David, 'Grasshopper Interface Explained,' 2015 <https://wiki.mcneel.com/labs/explicithistory/interfaceexplained> [accessed 6 June 2018]

Schumacher, Patrik, *The Autopoiesis of Architecture: A New Framework for Architecture* (Wiley, Chichester, 2011)

———, *The Autopoiesis of Architecture, Volume II: A New Agenda for Architecture* (Wiley, Chichester, 2012)

———, 'The Historical Pertinence of Parametricism and the Prospect of a Free Market Urban Order,' in *The Politics of Parametricism: Digital Technologies in Architecture*, ed. by Mathew Poole and Manuel Shvartzberg (Bloomsbury Academic, London and New York, 2015)

Shaviro, Steven, 'Against Self-Organization,' *The Pinocchio Theory*, 2009 <http://www.shaviro.com/Blog/?p=756> [accessed September 2013]

Taleb, Nassim Nicholas, *The Black Swan: The Impact of the Highly Improbable* (Random House, New York, 2007)

Terzidis, Kostas, *Permutation Design: Buildings, Texts, and Contexts* (Routledge, Abingdon, 2015)

Winchester, Simon, *The Perfectionists: How Precision Engineers Created the Modern World* (HarperCollins, New York, 2018)

3
IN DEFENSE OF PARTS

Optimizing for the many

> The designer becomes a designer of generating systems—each able of generating many objects—rather than the designer of individual objects.[1]

Since the introduction of nonstandardization to the field of architecture, we have seen a diminishing interest in the work of serialized units as a design strategy. Within nonstandard design, every building block has become different, as enabled by digital fabrication technologies and CNC manufacturing. As presented in Chapter 2, the dissolution of parts has increased design freedom through a larger formal repertoire but has done this by reducing market diversity and increasing the barrier of entry for new voices in the field. The continuous paradigm, in its capacity for trickle-down ephemeralization, has been the winning model for most of the current technological development which seeks to do "more with less" and allow for a more profitable model for corporate growth.

Parametric practice has developed a practical framework for an approach to architecture that views architecture as a singular, highly customized building that caters to the accumulation of wealth. Yet in parallel it has left open the field for designing a framework for the multitudes of buildings that make up the majority of our built environment. The ambitions of such a framework need to be able to address a larger portion of the architectural market and all non-market needs for architecture, encompassing professional and non-professional production. Such a framework should be described not only in terms of formal or technological principles but also in its capacity to be communicated and propagated among actors in the economy. The framework should also engage with ideas of openness and feedback mechanisms for adaptation, not as closed simulations that claim to engage with complexity like swarms but rather as socio-technical systems that are able to absorb contingent and variable requirements of the populations they serve.

This chapter will explore the study and development of the paradigm that was superseded by parametrics: the discrete paradigm. A reappraisal of discrete methodologies, augmented with contemporary technologies and a new critical understanding of the economics of inequality, can define an alternative, and far more inclusive, framework from that of parametric design. By reconsidering serial repetition in a new age of computation and network technologies, this chapter hopes to provide an alternative model that has the capacity to sustain a diverse multi-actor economy and challenge the coalition of larger design oligopolies.

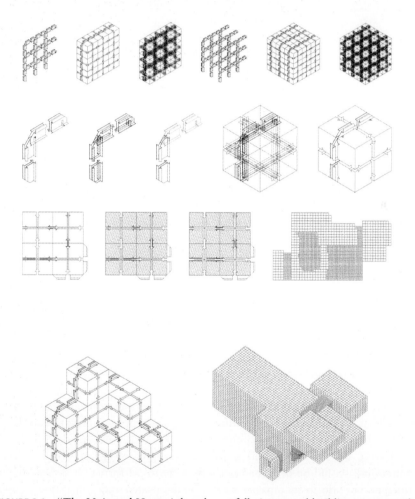

FIGURE 3.1   "The Universal House is based on a fully integrated building system made of self-interlocking discrete blocks which can be plugged in in any direction, as for the cladding panels." u-Cube/Universal House, Philippe Morel, 2009.

Discrete Architecture needs to establish foundational principles that go beyond an aesthetic of granularity. While Discrete Architecture can be studied through its contribution to a compositional lineage that can be traced back to De Stijl,[2] Le Modulor,[3] Field Conditions[4] and the Computationalism of Philippe Morel[5] (Figure 3.2), it has become more urgent to reconnect the formal and fabrication concerns of the discipline to the manner in which the discipline operates in and outside the market, allowing for collective strategies that might involve actors

FIGURE 3.2 Philippe Morel/EZCT Architecture & Design, Chair Model 'T1-M' after 860 generations (86,000 structural evaluations). "Studies on Optimization: Computational Chair Design using Genetic Algorithms (with Hatem Hamda and Marc Schoenauer)."

beyond competition. The proposition is to prioritize the collective starting from the production of tectonics that the field is so familiar with.

A market-driven architecture has sought to increase profit from optimization finding using techniques of vertical integration enabled by large accumulations of capital. Discrete Architecture can offer a different form of optimization, an optimization for the many, that seeks to reduce the barrier of entry and generate positive externalities in the form of combinatorial surplus from the production of design.

The studies of the discrete, then, will need to focus not only on the material performance or compositional freedoms offered by a geometric paradigm but also on the possibility of architecture and design as a form of local value production that rejects extractive practices aiming for the emergence of diverse idiosyncratic architecture and the increase of standards of living as social prosperity.

Discreteness beyond modularity

Discrete design is not a return to modularity. The modular and the discrete differ at an ontological and ideological level. As we will examine later, the modular movement was founded on how standardization can lead to a homogenization of industry producing large efficiencies in production. Discrete design, still in a stage of formalization, aims for a distributed and open-ended form of tectonic coordination, where families of compatible parts are able to define valuable patterns in their local context. Discrete is a movement of social participation, coordination and distributed value production with inevitable formal consequences to the constituent parts of buildings.

The notion of modularity popularized by Le Corbusier with "Modulor" in 1954[6] was understood both as a design system of proportions as well as project for standardization of building components. The adoption of a modular framework became an effort of dimensional coordination in the industry. Christine Wall has done a thorough anthropological study of the motivations and circumstances that led to the creation of the Modular Society in the 1950s, understanding the interest in establishing a mechanism of modular coordination and establishing industry standards for the reduction of the cost of buildings:

> The Modular Society campaigned for the universal dimensional coordination of construction components. This, it was argued, would reduce the wastage involved in traditional building, as modular structures would be built to order and fitted together on site. In turn, this would transform the construction process, from muddy chaos to clean and rational orderliness. The idea was a logical progression from pre-war prefabrication methods but instead of using a large range of different systems, the Modular Society promoted rationalization through a unified system of components, which would be chosen by the architect from a catalogue and fitted, ideally without any adjustment, on site.[7]

The Modular Society established a four-inch grid condition for industrialized parts. The modular was understood as the smallest indivisible dimension in a system of correlations or coordinates. While used for dimensioning material components, this grid condition antecedes any unit, as it is a property of space. It is a pre-established coordination aid for the arrangement of disparate elements.

Le Corbusier[8] and Walter Gropius[9] studied the implementation of modular frameworks based on the notion of human proportion to establish principles for the unequivocal combination of modules into meaningful wholes. These attempts were meant to generate a compositional unity that would demarcate order and an economic rationale for the optimal use of materials and space. Christine Wall identified that the Modular Society saw great potential in methodologies that would reduce the cost of buildings. Using this perspective, human scale influenced the design of building components through an evaluation of the efficiency of labor. As she explains:

> The object of the new Society will be to contribute toward lowering the cost of building by coordinating dimensions of materials, components and fittings on a modular basis. At present we are not getting full advantage of flow-production because standard and customary sizes of different components do not fit together.[10]

The inherent pursuit of optimizing and increasing revenue is intrinsic to all capitalist enterprises. However, there is something valuable to be understood in a project of coordination, as it bears the seeds for collaborative production. The problem of modularity has less to do with its ambitions for economic efficiency and more to do with its universality, which is predicated on the notion of the "average man."

While the modular project seeks to establish a framework for unity, the discrete paradigm seeks to establish a framework for diversity. The discrete emerges as a way to consider serial repetition that utilizes the economics of standardization without the universal framework of modularity. Central to the discrete is the coordination of different stakeholders in the economy and the development of open standards for compatibility and coproduction.

Discreteness is not a property of space as modularity is but a property of compatibility; e.g., a property of links. The construction of a discrete framework aims to reconsider parts and their relation with a totality, placing at the foreground the autonomy of units over superimposed structures such as a modular grid. Such a framework needs to allow incoherence, or the lack of compatibility between families of units. This is inevitable and celebrated, as no universal framework should override the possibility for the emergence of local codes of meaning and value. The framework trades economic efficiency for redundancy and open-endedness, understanding that it is impossible to forecast the value systems that might make a design pattern relevant.

Less than systems

Systems offer a functional understanding of parts and their relations. As has been explained by architect Christopher Alexander, the word "system" encapsulates two internal meanings that need to be distinguished. As he explained,

> In order to speak of something as a System, we must be able to state clearly: (1) The Holistic behaviour we are focusing on; (2) The parts within the thing, and the interaction among these parts, which cause the holistic behaviour we have defined; (3) The way in which this interaction among these parts, causes the holistic behaviour defined.[11]

For Alexander, there is a distinction between the holistic properties of the system and the generative ruleset defined by the kit of parts. He uses the term "generative system" to identify the latter, and he describes it as follows:

> We may generalize the notion of a generative system. Such a system will usually consist of a kit of parts (or elements) together with rules of combining them to form "allowable" things. The formal systems of mathematics are systems in this sense. The parts are numbers, variables, and signs like + or −. The rules specify ways of combining these parts to form expressions, ways of forming expressions from other expressions, and ways of forming true sentences, hence theorems of mathematics. Any combination of parts which is not formed according to the rules is either meaningless or false.[12]

From this perspective, discrete design engages with the development of generative systems but drops the requirement of those parts to acquire their meaning from holistic relations. Discrete design identifies a kit of parts, i.e., an initially finite set that allows for a multiplicity of assemblies, and places special emphasis on maintaining assemblies open-ended; aiming to couple the combinatorial potential of parts with social systems that can define patterns. While in technical terms, the definition of the set is finite, it is also open-ended as new social agents are able to introduce new parts expanding the combinatorial surplus of the set.

As established in Chapter 2, parametric design has co-opted the rhetoric of complex adaptive systems (CAS) that use bottom-up phenomena to remain open, generating adaptable designs. However, CAS simulations often only live in a closed environment, where computation is deterministic. Without a feedback mechanism, like the input of a social system, these simulations remain examples of deterministic top-down design. No input can alter the pre-established syntax of a parametric model. On the other hand, discrete design makes explicit a protocol for coordination, often via standardized joinery, allowing for new units to alter the definition of a whole.

The open-ended nature of discrete assemblies can be understood through the distinction between open and closed systems as presented by Ludwig von Bertalanffy.

Bertalanffy distinguishes an open system simply verifying the existence of external feedback, a mechanism that allows the system to self-regulate and maintain itself in a dynamic equilibrium.[13] As explained by Bertalanffy, the notion of an open system has properties of equifinality, understood as the property of reaching a given state through different means. The notion of a state in a system is the condition where holistic properties emerge. This is what Alexander calls a holistic behavior. In order for discrete design to further dismantle the necessity of a whole as a fixed condition or state, it is necessary to explore alternative mereological models of wholeness. It is possible to consider an assembly in a far more dynamic state, where units remain autonomous.

Holistic and non-holistic sets

Most traditional architecture uses a hybrid approach between discrete and continuous techniques: metal beams and bolts (discrete) or concrete (continuous). Most available materials come from a serialized chain of industrial production, allowing designers and architects to mix and match to develop cohesive wholes out of thousands of parts. Utilizing digital information models, the current design paradigm conceives of architecture in an abstract, pre-material state. It is only through a process of iterative post-rationalization that the architect, together with many other specialists, breaks this model and defines the constituent parts. The "whole" reaches its completion in abstraction usually through digital means and starts to be actualized through a process of decomposition where every part is fully detailed to fit into the larger model of the whole, what is denominated as a process of post-rationalization. As we have pointed out in Chapter 2, such a model resembles a jigsaw puzzle, meaning that each part only fits into one unique role in the assembly, serving a subservient role to the whole. Under this paradigm of post-rationalization, the topology of the system, the way in which parts connect to one another, is a rigid body map. We will define the model as "holistic sets," or collections of parts

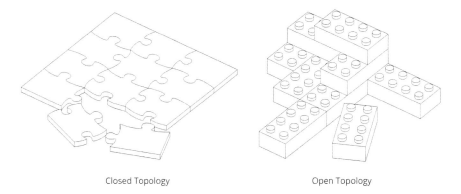

Closed Topology   Open Topology

FIGURE 3.3   Holistic set (jigsaw puzzle) vs non-holistic set (LEGO).

that operate under the ruling of the whole. In this model, the whole is fixed and unalterable.

Parametric software allows for the manipulation of the formal whole, emphasizing the "one-off" condition of an architectural proposition at every scale. Holistic sets define the capability of the whole to completely reinvent the parts in each architectural commission, if necessary. While this model offers great opportunity for performative geometries, it dismisses the opportunity for the reusability of building elements in different contexts. All architects develop their own vocabulary and do not engage with the vocabulary of others. There is no common language.

On the other hand, we can understand non-holistic sets as sets of parts that have a multiplicity of topological configurations. From this description, a non-holistic set also redefines the characteristics of the whole as remaining in a state of openness. These new emergent assemblies could be denominated "open-wholes" in their resistance of a static totality. A non-holistic set can be assimilated to a "kit of parts," which is in opposition to the jigsaw puzzle model discussed earlier under the paradigm of parametric design. Kits of parts have been popularized with products such as LEGO. While a particular LEGO product will contain the specific pieces to be assembled into one final structure, LEGO as a system is a non-holistic set. Parts are not designed to describe a unique whole, but rather to establish a systemic relationship with one another. The value of a non-holistic set is not defined by the materialization or actualization of the units but by their combinatorial capability. In this way, a discrete set defines a form of "combinatorial surplus" that is encapsulated in the potential encounters and degree of compatibility from one part with other parts.

MIT Professor and Director of the Center for Bits and Atoms Neil Gershenfeld has pioneered an understanding of discrete systems in his search for a universal building machine that can arrange units at a microscopic level. His interest in systems that could both assemble and disassemble objects follows principles of discrete reversibility. He has argued that while the reality of fabrication has embraced digital technologies to reach what we call today "digital fabrication," materials themselves have remained analog, as they still operate under the continuous paradigm of infinitesimal degrees of error. Gershenfeld would go ahead and describe and patent what he calls "digital materials." He explains:

> Digital parts are error correcting and self-aligning, which allows them to be assembled into structures with higher accuracy than the placement accuracy of the assembling person or machine. For example, a Lego™ set consists of discrete parts that have a finite number of joints. The male/female pin joints on the top and bottom of the Lego™ block are discrete connections, which either make or do not make a connection to another block. By contrast, a masonry construction is a continuous (analog) material; While the masonry brick is a discrete unit, the mortar in its fluid state allow one brick to be placed on top of another in an infinite number of positions. Because the joint is not discrete, masonry construction is analog while Lego™ construction is digital.[14]

Gershenfeld's research on digital materials points to a future where form can be patterned by "discrete assemblers,"[15] e.g., 3-D printing machines that do not extrude plastic but rather place small units of material together. Gershenfeld's work demonstrates how technologies that have transitioned from analog to digital, starting with communications based on Claude Shannon's seminal work, "A Mathematical Theory of Communication." Computation also experiences this transition from analog to digital during the 1950s. Gershenfeld explains how materiality, when controlled by digital fabrication, has remained analog, and that it is only the advent of digital materials that can establish a breakthrough toward a true digital architecture.

The supremacy of wholes and totalities is a mereological problem, as has been stated by architects Daniel Köhler and Rasa Navasaityte, who understand the

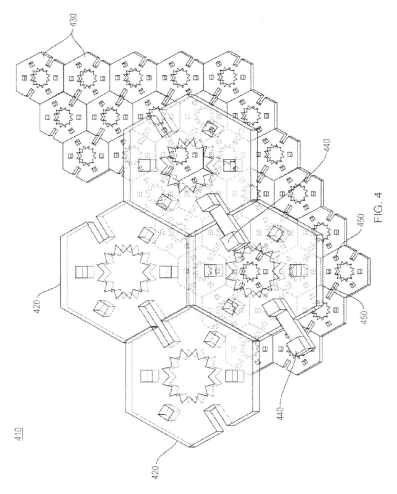

FIGURE 3.4   3-D model of hierarchical hexagonal press-fit structure, in "Additive Assembly of Digital Materials," by Jonathan Ward, MIT Center for Bits and Atoms.

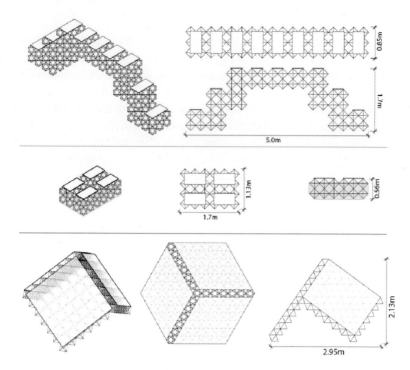

FIGURE 3.5   Digital material structure case studies. Configurations in the form of a bridge, boat and shelter. Drawings presented in axonometric, top and side view. Research project by Benjamin Jenett, Daniel Cellucci, Christine Gregg and Kenneth Cheung.

FIGURE 3.6   Logic Matter by Skylar Tibbits, MIT. Logic Matter is a system of passive mechanical digital logic modules for self-guided assembly of large-scale structures.

necessity to study buildings as part-to-whole relationships. Köhler and Navasaityte argue that "mereology, as opposed to typology, is a methodological framework for designing an architectural object not through a reference to its content or form, but through the resonance of its parts."[16]

Within a discrete framework, the autonomy of units increases, assemblies of multiple units start exhibiting differences from the wholes defined within holistic sets and wholes become more flexible and imbued with uncertainty. If units are designed with an awareness of systemic relations with one another, but not defining a unique topological diagram, parts acquire a degree of autonomy, as they could belong to a multiplicity of assemblies (perhaps the term "whole" loses its meaning). Units only need to be aware of their possible interface with other parts through a standard connection or link. The assembly of a multiplicity of parts could define the whole, but here again, the whole needs to be understood not as a final state but as a transient state of equilibrium, value or meaning. The organization of parts describing such an assembly defines a pattern, described by the information that determines the arrangement of a discrete set of parts.

Developed by philosopher and computer scientist Ian Bogost, the concept of "unit operations" can offer a powerful framework for conceptualizing parts as autonomous units operating as multitudes, acquiring meaning and value and acquiring unique patterns. For Bogost, the interplay of units is not necessarily tied to a holistic totality. Units are, and should, remain autonomous, allowing for spontaneous couplings that acquire meaning and value. As Bogost explains:

> I will suggest that any medium—poetic, literary, cinematic, computational—can be read as a configurative system, an arrangement of discrete, interlocking units of expressive meaning. I call these general instances of procedural expression unit operations.[17]

For Bogost, meaning emerges from the coupling of units without belonging to a larger holistic system. He describes units through their autonomy to a larger structure rather than parts of a whole. His distinction between wholes and multitudes allows for the existence of units without any overarching structure. Bogost writes:

> [A] world of unit operations hardly means the end of systems. Systems seem to play an even more crucial role now more than ever, but they are a new kind of system: the spontaneous and complex result of multitudes rather than singular and absolute holisms.[18]

The patterns that define such configurations are described as a temporal condition, e.g., one of a contingent of performative configurations. Bogost also explains the struggle that units need to maintain their individuation:

> Unit-operational systems are only systems in the sense they describe collections of units, structured in relation to one another. However, as Heidegger's suggestion advises, such operational structures must struggle to maintain their openness, to avoid collapsing into totalizing systems.[19]

The tectonic aggregate that is defined by unit operations can be described as a granular assembly, one that lives in opposition to the seamless continuity of a parametric style. Granular assemblies celebrate a collective condition that originated out of a multiplicity of origins. Architecture projects that have advanced the notion of discrete granular assemblies include Bloom by Jose Sanchez and Alisa Andrasek (Figures 3.7 and 3.8) and the Tallinn 2017 Architecture Biennial Pavilion by Gilles Retsin (Figures 3.9 and 3.10). These projects are defined by autonomous units that can be arranged in a multiplicity of configurations.

The visible granularity is a result of operating with the geometry of flatness; flatness offers a geometrical common language among units that have not been designed as a holistic system. Parts within a project are often only compatible with each other, defining a rigid protocol for compatibility. This protocol defines a limitation that has been circumvented through a number of design strategies. In the case of Bloom, units are slightly flexible, allowing for larger organizations to bend the rules of aggregation. Retsin, in his project Blockhut (Figure 3.11), envisions a hybrid model, where 90% of units are serially repeated discrete tectonics, while 10% of units can follow a logic of mass customization.[20] Finally, designers Golan Levin and Shawn Sims detected the incompatibility issues between different discrete building toys such as LEGO, DUPLO or Fischertechnik. Their design of the "Free Universal Construction Kit" (Figures 3.12 and 3.13) defines a matrix of connectors that establish compatibilities between otherwise incompatible sets. His

FIGURE 3.7 Bloom the Game by Jose Sanchez and Alisa Andrasek. The project is an open-ended building system made out of identical units. The formations of the project are created by the crowds that engage with them.

FIGURE 3.8   Bloom the Game by Jose Sanchez and Alisa Andrasek. Kids interacting with the piece for the London 2012 Olympic Games.

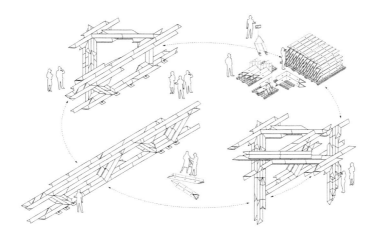

FIGURE 3.9   Diagram of discrete parts and proposals for a multiplicity of design assemblies based on the combinatorics of the system. Gilles Retsin Architecture, Tallinn Architecture Biennale Installation, 2017.

FIGURE 3.10 Tallinn Architecture Biennale installation composed of discrete units by Gilles Retsin Architecture, 2017.

Photo credit by NAARO.

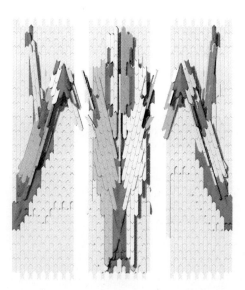

FIGURE 3.11 Diagram of hybrid model with discrete identical units (white) and bespoke units (gray).

Source: Gilles Retsin Architecture, Blokhut, 2015.

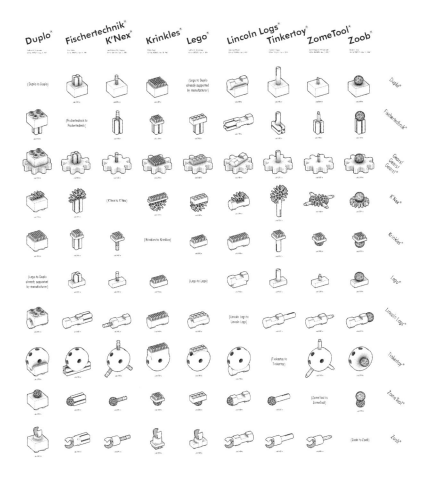

FIGURE 3.12 "Free Universal Construction Kit" by Golan Levin and Shawn Sims. Matrix of connections between different families of discrete units.

FIGURE 3.13 "Free Universal Construction Kit" by Golan Levin and Shawn Sims. Assembly connecting units from multiple sets.

project reflects on the open-ended nature of discrete granular assemblies, where new actors in the economy are able to expand on the universe of parts and increase the possibility space of combinations.

Granular assemblies also resist a tendency toward coalescence that would consolidate an assembly into a totality. Only by maintaining principles of reversibility, as has been understood in the tradition of dismountable architecture, can design patterns remain adaptable and flexible to the ever-changing landscape of the built environment.

Discrete design seeks to allow for such a condition of granular assemblies, or open-wholes that do not need to engage with systemic relations conforming to a performative state. This granularity is both literal and metaphorical, as it determines an architectural tectonic condition of units designed to exist in a multiplicity of contexts, and the result respects the provenance of contributions of all the agencies that took part in its production without pointing to a singular hierarchical author.

The geometrical data structures of links (links to unknown)

A new reading of mereological discourse has been invigorated by the work of philosopher Levi Bryant. Bryant develops the notion of a flat ontology while discussing the relations of parts to a whole. Flat ontology refers to a lack of hierarchy between units, attempting to conceptualize objects as possessing a fundamental autonomy between one another.[21] In holistic sets, what dictates the relationships between the parts is a hierarchical relation to the whole. The discrete paradigm resonates closer with the ideas presented by Bryant, where each unit, defined with its own autonomy, can operate in relation to other parts in a multiplicity of scenarios. An approach for discrete design needs to be able to identify and capitalize on this simple principle: a unit could be designed with its own autonomy in mind, anticipating and maximizing the millions of speculative encounters with other units. The unit is capable of establishing relations with other units but is not defined by its relationality.

To illustrate the ontology of an open-ended discrete system we will use as an example the Braun Lectron Kit (Figure 3.14), a pedagogical system developed in 1966. The Braun Lectron is a building set for electronics. The system uses principles of electrical engineering to allow a non-expert user to experiment and create sophisticated operational assemblies. The Braun Lectron kit was a discrete set of electric units, each of them containing a series of magnetic connections that would allow them to snap to each other via flat magnetic faces. The set contains functional units belonging to a generic electric system, such as resistors, modulators or speakers. The product is described as follows:

> Lectron is an electronic learning and experimentation system. It consists of standardized modules with magnetic contacts. Each Lectron-block contains an electronic component or a connecting line. Through meaningful juxtaposition of blocks arise functional circuits with standard-compliant diagrams.[22]

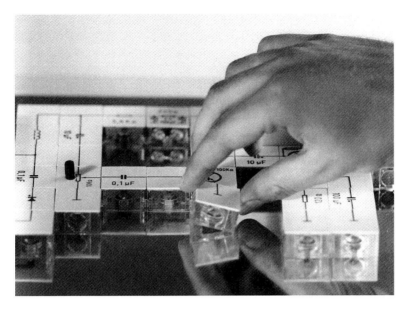

FIGURE 3.14 Braun Lectron System by Georg Gregor, 1960s. The kit offers a series of building blocks for electronics that can be combined using a magnetic connection.

Source: Image courtesy by Michael Peters

FIGURE 3.15 Braun Lectron System by Georg Gregor, 1960s. The kit offers a series of building blocks for electronics that can be combined using a magnetic connection.

Source: Image courtesy by Michael Peters

While no unit could do much on its own, by arranging these "electronic dominos" into a specific pattern, a user—often a child—would be able to construct a functional system, such as a radio. The radio configuration is one of the many recipes offered to users to learn how to combine units into different arrangements. Functional configurations might only use a subset of units from the kit, as all pieces are not needed to make a whole. This approach lends itself to the discovery of new patterns by both expert and non-expert users. Units can only achieve autonomy if they are designed with a multiplicity of scenarios in mind. As is the case with many discrete systems, in the case of the Braun Lectron kit, there is special attention given to the properties of the joint. The standardized joint establishes a protocol of communication and compatibility between units. While the anatomy of a unit can change greatly, the principles of the joint need to remain the same.

The Braun Lectron kit has been an innovative product that has greatly influenced the development of contemporary toys such as Little Bits (Figure 3.16 and 3.17) by Ayah Bdeir or robotic kits such as Cublets or Moss by Modular Robotics. In the case of Little Bits, we see the development of an entire language of parts that establish their own grammatical patterning. Here joints are also standardized, but the anatomy of the modules allow them to break free from the grid configuration previously presented by the Lectron Kit. This doesn't make Little Bits any less discrete, as discreteness does not imply a repetitive or uniform pattern of aggregation. On the contrary, it identifies that discreteness is fundamentally a protocol of

FIGURE 3.16 Little Bits, designed and created by Ayah Bdeir. The toy is an Open Source library of modular electronics that snap together using magnets.

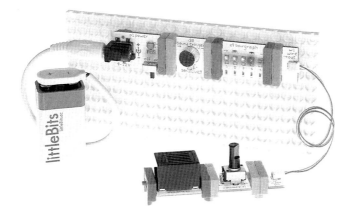

FIGURE 3.17 Little Bits, designed and created by Ayah Bdeir. Little Bits, operating as a discrete system, relies in the combinatorial possibilities discovered by crowds to design electronics.

connectivity and compatibility between parts that are strangers. These examples further advance the notion of "combinatorial surplus" as a value proposition of parts, defined not in their implemented relationality but in a potential relationality that is open to unexpected couplings.

Projects such as the Braun Lectron Kit, linked to Gershenfeld's notion of digital materials, start to define a fundamental distinction between the legacy practice of discreteness—e.g., standardized screws, beams, timber—and the new practice of digital discrete that is aware of the capacity of geometry to define a data structure. Each unit establishes a series of possible indexical relations to other units, allowing for the computation of a body map starting at any point of the network. In contrast to the parametric model, which utilizes an extrinsic data structure, the discrete model is in itself a data structure, offering the opportunities for data modeling operations and potentially local behaviors without a centralized form of control.

An example of this has been the adoption of voxel structures as spaceframes in architecture. Voxels are three-dimensional arrays of data, often understood as three-dimensional pixels. The data structure establishes a series of expected rules, like the neighboring conditions that a unit can have. In the case of an orthogonal voxel, each unit will always have 26 neighbors unless the unit is in an edge condition. Here the problem of conceptualizing data structures prior to units takes us closer to the notion of the whole. Data structures operate as a protocol of a potential whole, rather than predetermining its outcome. They allow the notion of the whole to remain in an open-ended condition.

There is a specific data structure that is flexible enough to establish the foundations of what we have been describing as Discrete Architecture: the graph.

A graph is constituted between nodes and edges. A node is able to establish any number of relations with other nodes represented by an edge or line between them. The edge implies a protocol of compatibility, or a relation established between units. Any form of Discrete Architecture should be able to be diagrammed using graphs, where elements are described as nodes and linkages are represented by edges. From this perspective, we are starting to reveal a picture of Discrete Architecture that develops the notion of "indexical parts," i.e., parts that are within functional patterns. Patterns contain the principles of a data structure and are able to identify which part belongs where, and how each part relates to other parts. Emerging from the structure of an assembly, the index defines the autonomy of a pattern as an information construct.

The work of Ben Jenett and Kenneth Cheung at the Center for Bits and Atoms at MIT, with their BILL-E robotic platform (Figure 3.18), sees discrete design as an opportunity for distributed robotics. The design of small robots that can navigate the structure they build, constituted of small discrete units, points out how discrete design offers an opportunity for automation. In architecture, The Research Cluster 4 at Bartlett School of Architecture in London, led by Gilles Retsin, Manuel Jimenez Garcia and Vicente Soler, aims to align discrete design with automation, designing units that consider the protocols of robotic assembly. In the work of their cluster (Figure 3.19), we see a move away from centralized robotic manufacturing and a turn toward distributed robotics. This move is also visible in the

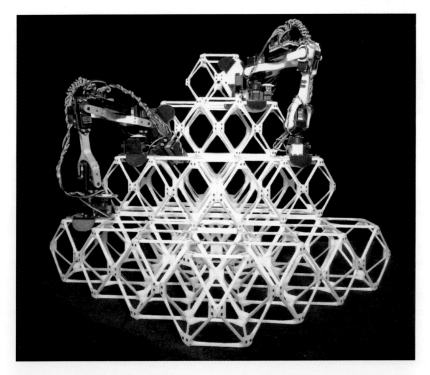

FIGURE 3.18   MIT Center for Bits and Atoms and NASA Ames Research Center. BILL-E robotic platform by Benjamin Jenett and Kenneth Cheung. Discrete lattice built by small distributed robotic system.

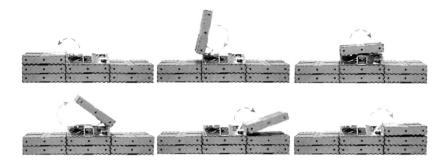

FIGURE 3.19   "PizzaBot (2018) is a fully autonomous construction system that explores possibilities for automation in the building sector. B-Pro Research Cluster 4, the Bartlett School of Architecture, UCL. Tutors: Gilles Retsin, Manuel Jimenez Garcia, Vicente Soler. Students: Mengyu Huang, Dafni Katrakalidi, Martha Masli, Man Nguyen, Wenji Zhang."

research "Distributed Robotic Assembly for Timber Structures" (Figure 3.20) led by Ramon Weber and Samuel Leder at the Institute of Computational Design and Construction in Stuttgart. These projects capture the distributed potential of discrete design, one in which multiple agents are able operate simultaneously. Nevertheless, exploiting the distributed nature of discrete design through automation reintroduces hierarchical control and misses the opportunity of allowing a discrete framework to remain open to for a multi-actor economy.

We still need to define how patterns emerge and acquire meaning from a design perspective. As the continuous paradigm utilizes parametric design to modulate and articulate the intensities of flows and surfaces, the discrete paradigm will need

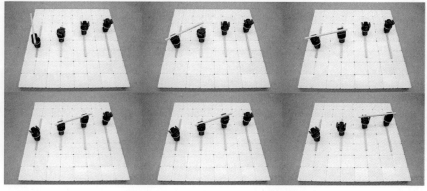

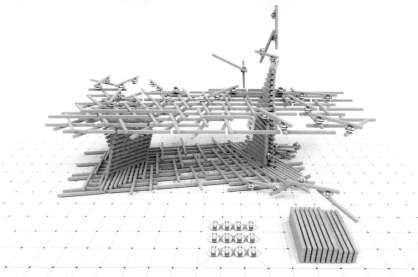

FIGURE 3.20   Ramon Weber, Samuel Leder, Distributed Robotic Assembly for Timber Structures, 2018.

to identify the design strategies to engage the patterning of units. This will be described here as combinatorial design.

Combinatorial design

As we shift our attention toward discrete design, operating with kits of parts and explicit linkages between them, the design process is altered. In the parametric design paradigm, design could be understood as a search function that operates moving in degree along an infinitesimal domain. Designing with discrete units doesn't allow a gradient flow between variables but combinatorial patterning instead. While a parametric definition can offer a multiplicity of designs, those alternatives offer difference in degree. A discrete methodology on the other hand, with its open-ended combinatorial possibilities, offers difference in kind. The Braun Lectron kit that we discussed earlier serves as a good example; different configurations of the units do not create variants of a radio but different functionalities altogether.

Coming from mathematics, the term combinatorics describes the studies of the structures allowed by a finite set of discrete units. In its definition, the term demarcates a difference from nonstandard calculus, identifying that it operates in the realm of the discrete rather than the continuous. It also denotes the use of "finite," countable units, as opposed to the variable units described by a parametric model.

The degree of differentiation of a parametric model can only operate by stretching and shrinking a fixed topological diagram. A combinatorial model lacks a topological diagram. One only arises as a contingent proposition unique to the pattern of arrangement. This is what can be called "the missing topology mechanic."[23] A pattern establishes the linkages and relations between units, defining the topological diagram of the model. These patterns are immaterial, as they are defined by the indexical information that links units. This information density stored in a design pattern can be characterized as a metric of order that differentiates the aggregation from pure randomness. The challenge of combinatorics is that of negative entropy, the creation of information-rich patterns.

It's important to be clear that combinatorial design is not just the study of possible permutations of parameters, or what Kostas Terzidis calls "permutation design,"[24] where any given variable of a design problem establishes a degree of freedom that can be catalogued and cross-referenced to other variables, yielding the solution space of a given system. In fact, Terzidis rejects how intuition and experience can play a role in the design process, favoring a framework of optimization performed by a deep search of algorithms over the permutation space. He explains:

> Traditionally, such arrangements are done by human designers who base their decision making either on intuition (from the point of view of the designer) or on random sampling until a valid solution is found. However, in both cases the solution found may be an acceptable one but cannot be labeled as "the best possible solution" due to the subjective or arbitrary nature of the selection process. In contrast, an exhaustive list of permutation-based arrangements will eventually reveal the "best solution" since it will exclude all other possible solutions.[25]

In comparison to Terzidis, combinatorial design is a design strategy that starts from the definition and individuation of parts, describing an open-ended series of relations with one another. These parts are coupled and aggregated to generate larger assemblies, describing meaning, performance and function at different scales of configuration. The system always remains open-ended and malleable, allowing for the replacement of parts within it. The open-endedness of the system implies that there is no possible optimization, as the solution space of permutations grows with each unit added at an exponential rate, becoming computationally impossible to search for an optimum. The malleability of a combinatorial system implies a temporal relevance and the contingent emergence of a pattern out of contextual conditions. No pattern might be the optimal one for a long period of time but rather an ad hoc solution harvested by designers or as we will see in the following chapter, crowds.

Combinatorial design can define a broader scope for a design agenda that is interested in developing a common repository of architectural units with potential compatibilities. A discrete combinatorial methodology is a project of coordination between different design entities aiming to generate positive externalities from the contribution of a publicly accessible catalog of architectural knowledge.

Design as patterns

The implications of reconsidering a distributed mass production of units that operate under combinatorics are not only formal, but socioeconomical. It's important to note that the framework described here is not an attempt to describe the "nature" of design but rather a conscious attempt to design a framework for social cooperation, developing the thesis that combinatorial surplus is a value proposition that designs down the barrier of entry on new designers and offers exponential opportunities for socially appropriated innovation. While the design of units requires high technical knowledge, considering principles of engineering and fabrication, patterns, understood as the production of granular assemblies through the combination of units, belong to an iterative, even playful, form of design speculation, where the combinations of already established units can yield a diversity of results with varying degrees of social relevance. While it might seem pertinent that there is a symbiosis between the production of units and the development of patterns, the search space offered by all the possible combinations between units offers the opportunity of open design to non-expert users, generating a feedback loop into the system and generating design literacy along the way.

There have been two central areas of research that are able to contribute in the production of valuable patterns: artificial intelligence and crowds. In the case of artificial intelligence, algorithms are used to search for patterns that perform under specific criteria. An AI algorithm might not necessarily understand what makes a pattern meaningful but will establish correlations of value by learning from large training data sets. While this technique might be able to replicate, adapt and even find patterns that have not yet been acknowledged, it lacks any feedback mechanism with the production of culture itself, which is the engine that determines what is meaningful for a particular social system. An AI, bound by its domain, as discussed in Chapter 2 and described by the Black Swan, is blind to phenomena that escape the solution space. Here is where the engagement of crowds can offer an open-ended proliferation of patterns. The process of value production is coupled with cultural adoption, so it is only natural that the production and utilization of patterns would benefit from this social coupling.

At this point it is important to note that the coupling of discrete combinatorial design with social systems could offer radically different connotations. One perspective would encourage crowd harvesting, utilizing centralized forms of data collection where social engagement is equated to free labor. This position is profoundly problematic and fundamentally aligned to the neoliberal practices described in Chapter 1. The position that will be developed here and throughout Chapter 5 is aligned to the production of the Commons, where social production acquires local cultural value in the hands of the members engaging with the labor. The output of such production is also expected to remain in the communities that produce it.

Unlike Alexander's formalization of design patterns as finite, static and timeless,[26] design patterns are framed here as flexible, mutable and highly idiosyncratic. Patterns are the formalization of a temporal configuration of units. Patterns offer a form of weak and open-ended holism that does not dictate the require performance or role of parts. This is what Timothy Morton calls "subscendence wholes,"[27] where the whole is not more than the sum of its parts but less. Morton doesn't deny the existence of the whole but suggests that parts always exceed the totality:

> Very well, a tree exists in the same way as a forest. The forest is ontologically one. The trees are more than one. The parts of the forest (the trees—but there is so many more parts in fact) outnumber the whole. This doesn't mean they "are more important than the whole." This is the kind of anti-holistic reductionism that neoliberalism promotes: "There is no such thing as society; there are only individuals." We need holism, but a special, weak holism that isn't theistic.[28]

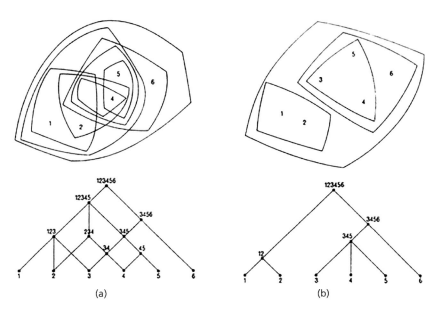

FIGURE 3.21   Semi-Lattice Structure used by Christopher Alexander in "The City is not a Tree" in 1965. Diagrams redrawn by Nikos Salingaros, copyright Christopher Alexander and the Center for Environmental Structure.

In Morton's view, an object can always belong to multiple wholes as part of what could be described as a mesocosm; a blurry boundary where objects come and go.[29] Like Morton, Alexander challenged the interpretation that the city (Alexander's object, or "whole" of study) was indeed a hierarchy, or a tree.[30] The tree suggests a neatly hierarchical pattern where order is nested at identifiable layers. Alexander suggests that the city should be understood as a semi-lattice; a structure with multiple overlapping groupings, where units would belong to a multiplicity of partial wholes.

Alexander's semilattice structure offers a powerful visual representation of a complex non-hierarchical groupings. What is not challenged by such a structure is subservience of parts to the functional whole. Morton, on the other hand, offers a version of partial objects, an alteration of the meaning of holism where the parts are able to exceed the whole to which they belong. What is described here as design patterns in the context of Discrete Architecture should be seen as an open-ended aggregate, with the potential for a multiplicity of sub-groupings where the parts resist the complete subscription to a totality.

Discreteness as a value proposition

What has been described as Discrete Architecture can be presented as a renewed interest in parts and the composition of wholes through the production of patterns. Discrete Architecture has important implications in the definition of form, but it holds the risk to be evaluated just as an aesthetic paradigm, much like parametrics.

As we will explore in the following chapter, the production of content can grow exponentially with the introduction of digital platforms. Non-expert users are able to engage with design through digital interfaces or video games that have been designed to educate and aid in the implementation of technical knowledge. But who profits from such production and what are the ethical imperatives of platform infrastructure in regard to users? It has not been the architectural field that has initiated a pushback toward contemporary inequality in identifying the Commons as an area of theory and in need for formal implementation; the acknowledgment and protection for the Commons has been a global project for many disciplines for decades, and a movement that seems to gain strength with the global understanding of the calamities perpetrated by a form of unregulated capitalism. As Negri and Hardt explain:

> Neoliberal government policies throughout the world have sought in recent decades to privatize the common, making cultural products—for example information, ideas and even species of animals and plants—into private property. We argue, in chorus with many others, that such privatization should be resisted.[31]

The production of valuable design patterns by a multitude requires the conceptualization and structural implementation of the Commons; a legally defined territory that can absorb and store the production of value. Architecture's role needs to be more clearly associated with the discipline's skills in the conceptualization, design and fabrication of models for equitable and inclusive cities, starting from the very fabric of its buildings.

The self-imposed constraint of using serializable parts does not follow a stylistic trend but rather seeks to encapsulate knowledge in physical objects, allowing for a democratization of design when opened to larger audiences through digital platforms. This might seem an arbitrary constraint, but behind it is a social and economic agenda that seeks to expand the role of architecture beyond market economics. This strategy shifts the production agency from high-stakes developers who hold large accumulations of wealth, toward multitudes that can generate collective iterations of contingent issues. This call is to hinder the model of knowledge protection by large actors in the economy and to facilitate a model of knowledge propagation, attempting to dismantle a "one-to-one" correlation between architects and buildings, allowing for an exponential proliferation of culturally relevant design patterns via the Commons.

The rise of inequality calls not only for political participation as citizens, but also a reformulation of our professional practice, examining our established practices for funding, labor and design objectives. In architecture, form and composition are not "off the hook" when we address our socio-political concerns. The field needs to be able to distinguish which strategies perpetuate a neoliberal landscape that divides and polarizes cities and the rest of our built environment. This is not to be misinterpreted as a regressive proposition that is attempting to go back to a time in which the discipline did not need to concern itself with issues of technology or fabrication. Discrete Architecture is an attempt to engage some of the most pervasive forms of technological governance and branch out parallel trajectories that place social progress ahead of a technological or compositional one.

As we will discuss in the next chapters, the production of the Commons and the attempts to protect them can be observed in formal developments concerning copyright and mechanisms for social organization. Technologies such as the General Purpose License (GPL) by Richard Stallman, Creative Commons Licenses and Open Source initiatives constitute organizational and legal innovations that allow an alternative trajectory for professional practice. The role of these innovations is fundamentally linked to the ability of individuals to organize themselves and develop protocols for sharing and governing the outputs of their collective labor. While the parametric design movement of the 1990s was facilitated by innovations due to calculus and the development of surfaces, today's technological advancements offer the capacity to connect people in a myriad of ways, many of them with the potential for exploitative extraction of capital. Architecture needs to acknowledge its role in the perpetuation of an economic model and discover avenues for alternatives.

Notes

1 Christopher Alexander, 'Systems Generating Systems,' *Architectural Design*, 7.6 (December 1968), 90–91.

2 Theo Van Doesburg, 'De Stijl, 1917–1928,' *De Stijl* (1952), MoMA museum catalogue, <https://www.moma.org/documents/moma_catalogue_1798_300159061.pdf>.

3 Le Corbusier, *The Modulor: A Harmonious Measure to the Human Scale Universally Applicable to Architecture and Mech* (MIT Press, 1977).

4 Stan Allen, *Points and Lines: Diagrams and Projects for the City* (Princeton Architectural Press, 1999).

5 Philippe Morel, 'On Computationalism,' in *EP: Design Fiction* (Sternberg Press, 2016), pp. 142–153.

6 Corbusier, *The Modulor*.

7 Christine Wall, *An Architecture of Parts: Architects, Building Workers and Industrialisation in Britain 1940–1970* (Routledge, 2013).

8 Corbusier, *The Modulor*.

9 Gilbert Herbert, *Dream of the Factory-Made House: Walter Gropius and Konrad Wachsmann* (MIT Press, 1984).

10 Wall, *An Architecture of Parts*.

11 Alexander, 'Systems Generating Systems.'

12 Alexander, 'Systems Generating Systems.'

13 Ludwig von Bertalanffy, *General System Theory: Foundations, Development, Applications* (George Braziller Inc, 1968).

14 Neil Gershenfeld and Jonathan Daniel Ward, 'Hierarchical Functional Digital Materials,' 1 (2013). <https://patents.google.com/patent/US20130189028>.

15 Jonathan Ward, *Additive Assembly of Digital Materials* (MIT Press, 2010).

16 Rasa Navasaityte and Daniel Koehler, 'Mereological Tectonics: The Figure and Its Figuration,' *TxA Emerging Technologies Proceedings* (2016), 1–14 <www.academia.edu/33092878/Mereological_Tectonics_The_Figure_and_its_Figuration>.

17 Ian Bogost, *Unit Operations: An Approach to Videogame Criticism, Unit Operations* (MIT Press, Cambridge, 2006).

18 Bogost, *Unit Operations*.

19 Bogost, *Unit Operations*.

20 Gilles Retsin, 'Discrete Assemblage as Design and Fabrication Strategy,' *TxA Emerging Technologies Proceedings* (2015), 98–103.

21 Levi R. Bryant, *The Democracy of Objects* (Michigan Publishing, University of Michigan Library, 2011).

22 Georg Gregor, 'Lectron–Elektronisches Lern- Und Experimentiersystem–Das Lectron Prinzip' (1965) <www.lectron.de/> [accessed 13 April 2014].

23 Jose Sanchez, 'Polyomino – The Missing Topology Mechanic,' in *ALIVE: Advancements in Adaptive Architecture,* ed. by Manuel Kretzer and Ludger Hovestadt (Birkhauser, Basel, 2014).

24 Kostas Terzidis, *Permutation Design: Buildings, Texts, and Contexts* (Routledge, 2015).

25 Terzidis, *Permutation Design*.

26 Christopher Alexander, *The Timeless Way of Building* (Oxford University Press, 1979).

27 Timothy Morton, *Humankind: Solidarity With Non-Human People* (Verso, 2017).

28 Morton, *Humankind*.

29 Morton, *Humankind*.

30 Christopher Alexander, 'A City Is Not a Tree,' *Architectural Forum,* 122.1 (April 1965), 58–62.

31 Michael Hardt and Antonio Negri, *Commonwealth* (Harvard University Press, 2009).

References

Alexander, Christopher, 'A City Is Not a Tree,' *Architectural Forum*, 122.1 (April 1965), 58–62.
———, 'Systems Generating Systems,' *Architectural Design* (Wiley, Chichester, December 1968), 90–91

————, *The Timeless Way of Building* (Oxford University Press, New York, 1979)

Allen, Stan, *Points and Lines: Diagrams and Projects for the City* (Princeton Architectural Press, New York, 1999)

Bertalanffy, Ludwig von, *General System Theory: Foundations, Development, Applications* (George Braziller, New York, 1968)

Bogost, Ian, *Unit Operations: An Approach to Videogame Criticism, Unit Operations* (MIT Press, Cambridge, 2006)

Bryant, Levi R., *The Democracy of Objects* (Michigan Publishing, University of Michigan Library, Ann Arbor, 2011)

Doesburg, Theo Van, 'De Stijl, 1917–1928,' *De Stijl* (1952), MoMA museum catalogue, https://www.moma.org/documents/moma_catalogue_1798_300159061.pdf [accessed November 2017]

Gershenfeld, Neil, and Jonathan Daniel Ward, 'Hierarchical Functional Digital Materials,' 1 (2013). <https://patents.google.com/patent/US20130189028> [accessed November 2017]

Gregor, Georg, 'Lectron–Elektronisches Lern- Und Experimentiersystem–Das Lectron Prinzip' (1965) <www.lectron.de/> [accessed 13 April 2014]

Hardt, Michael, and Antonio Negri, *Commonwealth* (Harvard University Press, Cambridge, 2009)

Herbert, Gilbert, *Dream of the Factory-Made House: Walter Gropius and Konrad Wachsmann* (MIT Press, Cambridge, 1984)

Le Corbusier, *The Modulor: A Harmonious Measure to the Human Scale Universally Applicable to Architecture and Mechanics*, (Massachusetts Institute of Technology Press, Cambridge, 1977)

Morel, Philippe, 'On Computationalism,' in *EP: Design Fiction* (Sternberg Press, Berlin, 2016), pp. 142–153

Morton, Timothy, *Humankind: Solidarity With Non-Human People* (Verso, London, 2017)

Navasaityte, Rasa, and Daniel Koehler, 'Mereological Tectonics: The Figure and Its Figuration,' *TxA Emerging Technologies Proceedings* (2016), 1–14

Retsin, Gilles, 'Discrete Assemblage as Design and Fabrication Strategy,' *TxA Emerging Technologies Proceedings* (2015), 98–103

Sanchez, Jose, 'Polyomino – The Missing Topology Mechanic,' in *ALIVE: Advancements in Adaptive Architecture,* ed. by Manuel Kretzer and Ludger Hovestadt (Birkhauser, Basel, 2014)

Terzidis, Kostas, Permutation Design: Buildings, *Texts, and Contexts* (Routledge, Abingdon, 2015)

Wall, Christine, *An Architecture of Parts: Architects, Building Workers and Industrialisation in Britain 1940–1970* (Routledge, Abingdon, 2013)

Ward, Jonathan, *Additive Assembly of Digital Materials* (Massachusetts Institute of Technology Press, Cambridge, 2010)

4

IMMATERIAL ARCHITECTURES

Surveillance, data collection and crowd-sourced labor

In his studies of digital economies, Professor Nick Srnicek has denominated the term "platform capitalism" as the current condition of how information is collected and monetized through the Internet.[1] According to Srnicek, data has become a new raw material that the recent form of 21st-century capitalism has been exploiting for years. To harvest this data, new infrastructural models needed to emerge. A platform facilitates interactions in a network, placing itself in a privileged and hierarchical position between users. As Srnicek explains, a platform has a unique position to record and collect data on any interactions occurring in the platform.

Corporations such as Facebook, YouTube or Google are examples of contemporary platforms, each possessing an asymmetric relation to all other users in their almost-monopolization of network infrastructure. YouTube's users are encouraged to promote and grow the network by becoming partners of the network, receiving payment from the views of content they create. This monetization establishes competition for the production of content, where users operate as entrepreneurs, building their channel and brand identity. For theorists such as Srnicek[2] and Tiziana Terranova,[3] this constitutes a business model based on the exploitation of free labor, i.e., "laborers who produce goods (data and content) that are then taken and sold by the companies to advertisers and other interested parties."[4]

Platforms are critical for the production of social content, and as we will discuss in this chapter, they present a crucial technology for the potential coordination between users. While in physical systems, discussed in Chapter 3, combinatorial design occurs with the direct engagement of available building blocks, in the medium of digital platforms it is possible to simulate and design information patterns prior to design execution. It is in this sense that platforms present a critical potential for the production of common repositories of knowledge, but the model and design of current platforms trends toward neoliberal exploitation, what Sho-shana Zuboff has denominated "surveillance capitalism." As she explains:

> It is important to note the vital differences for capitalism in these two moments of originality at Ford and Google. Ford's inventions revolutionized production. Google's inventions revolutionized extraction and established surveillance capitalism's first economic imperative: the extraction imperative. The extraction imperative meant that raw-material supplies must be pro-cured at an ever-expanding scale. Industrial capitalism had demanded econo-mies of scale in production in order to achieve high throughput combined with low unit cost. In contrast, surveillance capitalism demands economies of scale in the extraction of behavioral surplus.[5]

Zuboff identifies the key characteristics exhibited by digital platforms today: a neo-liberal practice of extractivism as we have discussed in Chapter 1 and a manipula-tion of crowds through behavioral surplus. The unregulated capability of platforms to engage in behavior modification is perhaps the most critical challenge for the design of technology today, as it is necessary to conceive of and design systems that not only avoid the exercise of such power but also dismantle the possibility of such illegitimate power to exist in the first place. Zuboff has made a critical point to anticipate the rise of "instrumentarian power" as a more pervasive form of sur-veillance that not only observes but also is able to alter human behavior, which in turn is monetized. As she explains: "[S]urveillance capitalists declare their right to modify others' behavior for profit according to methods that bypass human aware-ness, individual decision rights, and the entire complex of self-regulatory processes that we summarize with terms such as autonomy and self-determination."[6]

The current exercise of instrumentarian power observed by Zuboff has given rise to the erosion of democracy. While operating within a private platform, a user typically signs an agreement with the network provider to handle their data for the commercial use of the company. Following the whistleblower Christopher Wylie's denouncement of the data collection performed by Cambridge Analytica, the hear-ing of Mark Zuckerberg in front of a US congressional committee in April 2018 evidenced the lack of understanding of the general public and government regard-ing issues of privacy and data ownership. US Senator Richard Durbin said that he believes "that may be what this is all about. Your right to privacy. The limits of your right to privacy. And how much you give away in modern America in the name of, quote, connecting people around the world."[7]

The right to privacy is a battle that has long been fought by technology insid-ers, such as the group denominated as Cypherpunks, whose members include the Internet activist and creator of WikiLeaks Julian Assange. For Assange, the current state of platform capitalism is far bleaker than what we have been led to believe.

> The internet, our greatest tool of emancipation, has been transformed into the most dangerous facilitator of totalitarianism we have ever seen. The

internet is a threat to human civilization. These transformations have come about silently because those who know what is going on work in the global surveillance industry and have no incentives to speak out. Left to its own trajectory, within a few years, global civilization will be a postmodern surveillance dystopia, from which escape for all but the most skilled individuals will be impossible. In fact, we may already be there.[8]

His message is a call to arms for utilizing the power of encryption to protect the right of privacy. For Assange, the technology of encryption presents a unique possibility for limiting the capacity of platforms and states to breach the privacy of individuals. This assessment operates under the simple principle that it is easier to encrypt information than it is to decrypt. As Assange presents it:

> [T]he universe, our physical universe, has that property that makes it possible for an individual or a group of individuals to reliably, automatically, even without knowing, encipher something, so that all the resources and all the political will of the strongest superpower on earth may not decipher it. And the paths of encipherment between people can mesh together to create regions free from the coercive force of the outer state. Free from mass interception. Free from state control.
>
> Cryptography is the ultimate form of non-violent direct action.
>
> Strong cryptography can resist an unlimited application of violence. No amount of coercive force will ever solve a math problem.[9]

Assange calls for collective resistance that begins from the acknowledgment that the right to privacy is fundamental in order to protect democracy. His methods with WikiLeaks are an attempt to increase the literacy of data privacy issues through the public exposure of corrupt practices. WikiLeaks has been at the forefront of transparency advocacy, attempting to bring some light to the unseen power exerted by obfuscating networks. Through the advocacy of connecting people and giving voice to new members in democratized platforms, the Internet has created one of the most powerful infrastructures for mass surveillance. Today, there are those who are attempting to weaponize it for political agendas.

Platforms, in their current form, homogenize. User actions are constrained to a series of identifiable choices, allowing the gathered data to be comprehensively tabulated and analyzed for further monetization. Digital platforms are where patterns are created. Computation and the use of artificial intelligence has allowed the categorization of individuals from rigid stereotypes to one-of-a-kind data personas that can follow predictable consumer patterns. Far from offering an emancipatory medium for the proliferation of new value, surveillance platforms instrumentalize their knowledge to manufacture certainty and monetize predictions.[10] The interactions of millions of individuals constantly reshapes culture and redefines value. The design of alternative and critical platforms has become urgent. It is a design problem to reconceptualize these spaces where we spent time on in the Internet, challenging the market model of homogenization and attempting to redefine the ethos of a network as a fundamentally collaborative enterprise.

Access—transparency from surveillance

The failure of ephemeralization that we have discussed in Chapter 1 is the failure of the "trickle down" model of knowledge propagation. It has become urgent to dedicate at least an equal amount of effort to the problem of diffusion and implementation of new technologies as has been given to the problem of innovation. This was understood by Stewart Brand, who in 1968 founded and published the *Whole Earth Catalog*.[11] The *Catalog* was an initiative to share and propagate information about a wide variety of tools and techniques. Buckminster Fuller is listed as a contributor and inspiration for the publication. The *Whole Earth Catalog*, a mid-20th century publication, remains progressive in its approach. Much of its content is dedicated to smart geometries that minimize the use of materials or clever ways to harvest land. Its subtitle *Access to Tools* points to the importance of the distribution of knowledge and access to performance and quality through the items in the catalog. At the center of the *Whole Earth Catalog* was a principle that design is a distributed form of social recombination, one in which a large repository of objects and technologies available would be accessible to individuals for improving society at large. The legacy of the *Whole Earth Catalog* has been profound and far-reaching, influencing a large number of other publications and business strategies. However, it is perhaps only today, on the back of a new and invigorated DIY maker-movement, that one can refer back to the significance of its format, as an open-ended list for public recombination.

The problem of knowledge production and protection for it to remain accessible to the public has been an ongoing battle as the power of copyrights has grown over time. In 1989 Richard Stallman developed the General Purpose License (GPL).[12] The GPL was a response to what Stallman had identified as a problem that stifled the innovation and creativity of software developers. The problem was copyright laws and proprietary software. As economist Joseph Stiglitz has argued, there is no evidence that extensions of copyright laws have any benefit for innovation. Stiglitz categorized copyrights as property that does not generate additional value but extracts value as a rent.[13]

Stallman's proposition was to devise a legal license—the GPL—that would ensure that software or content developed licensed under it would remain free to be copied, modified and distributed. In the words of David Bollier: "Instead of locking the code up as private property, it ensures everyone the freedom to copy, modify or distribute a software program as they see fit, including to sell it at a price."[14]

Additionally, the GPL license had a recursive component, as any derivative work developed from a software licensed under the GPL would have to maintain a GPL licensing. In principle, this would provide a legal framework for the production and expansion of content in the public domain. As explained by Stallman, the emerging "free software" movement was not concerned with giving access for free but with the freedom of access.

Free software allows for public scrutiny of the extractive practices that software providers obfuscate behind the fine print of user agreements. By enabling access to the code of a software, members of the community are able to denounce features that violate the trust of users, features that if exposed publicly would deincentivize users to use that particular product. Not all users are expected to play this custodial role, but some will, and do. Without any public scrutiny or regulatory oversight, software becomes a black box: inaccessible and obfuscated from any public access. This leads for an opportunity to execute data extraction protocols for further commercialization.

While a closed copyrighted system currently is the format in which companies protect innovation, this mechanism restricts the free flow of knowledge to parties that could further advance the ideas put forward. This generates an artificial sense of scarcity. The stifling of innovation has occurred for years, as companies sit on patents and do not develop the patents' technology further. This has been the case with the 3-D printing revolution that had to wait for years for the patents of plastic extrusion to expire, eventually allowing for a myriad of companies to look at 3-D printing from several different perspectives. The openness of software offers a key advantage in the propagation of knowledge. In the words of Joseph Stiglitz: "Abusing the patent system is another avenue for reducing competition. Patents are a temporary barrier to entry."[15]

The argument behind copyrights is that by granting exclusive right of access and protection from competitors, the market incentivizes innovation. But patents have lost their original intent to operate as an incentive and have become a legal tool, used and abused to dismantle competitors. As Stiglitz argues, large corporations own thousands of patents that they allow each other to use, constructing serious defense against new entrants.[16]

The usefulness of patents is predicated in an economic framework of corporate competition where continuous innovation is the tool for market advantage. Yet this is not the only model of innovation out there. Eric von Hippel offers the framework of "free innovation" to describe the innovation done by users without a commercial interest. Von Hippel's studies demonstrate that the model of free innovation lives in parallel to that of producer innovation and is able to operate in a far more organic and inclusive way.[17] Von Hippel's distinction identifies a different motivation for the pursuit of innovation. While producer innovation seeks to maintain a competitive advantage, the self-organizing peer-to-peer production that characterizes free innovation is always linked to a form of value production, where wealth remains in the network.[18]

Discrete Architecture and the combinatorial framework presented in Chapter 3 seek to accelerate and provide design theory for von Hippel's free innovation paradigm, allowing parts to become a vehicle for the propagation of knowledge. In this paradigm, the performance of a part is not evaluated by its singular performance toward an output but rather as the social performance to contribute to a multiplicity of scenarios, what we have denominated "combinatorial surplus." The part may be suboptimal for one design context but offer multi-context performance.

An analogy can be found in the evolution and growth of the popularity of certain programming languages. The proliferation of different programming languages in the last 30 years has allowed for a myriad of different design paradigms. Some of these allow for modularity and the possibility of re-combination. The paradigm of Object-Oriented Programming (OOP) has become one of the most widely adopted programming paradigms for its capacity to develop autonomous and reusable objects. In an OOP paradigm, code is structured to define objects, or entities that have a definition independent of the context in which they may interact. These objects can be defined with a series of public and private variables that determine the access that other objects will be granted in a given interaction. The OOP paradigm is interested in the way objects can relate with one another through libraries, or lists of objects previously developed by other developers.

The value of the paradigm appears once a designer has accumulated a library of objects, accelerating their ability to respond to a new scenario and increasing exponentially the possible combinations between already created digital objects. Objects become custom tools for a designer. Their reusability becomes a valuable resource over time. This value is further amplified when pools of objects are made available for the use of others. The incentive for a developer to share the content they have produced with a network is based on the value acquired when all other members of the network have done the same. The result is a non-zero sum game, where everyone can benefit from the exponential capacity of recombination of self-contained objects. Designers who have engaged with programming, and in particular OOP languages, develop a profound understanding of the inheritance of knowledge, as software and code is always an aggregate of virtual objects and ideas that have been developed by others. This aggregate is not a collage where pieces are mashed together but rather a careful combinatorial pattern of discrete units.

In the context of OOP, objects constitute the building blocks for a form of social recombination. These phenomena could be studied and understood through the lens of the Processing.org community. Processing, a programming language developed by Ben Fry and Casey Reas,[19] builds upon the work of John Maeda and many others at MIT who have sought to increase the literacy of programming by reducing the complexity that is faced by those learning how to code. The Processing environment places importance on the proliferation of design through the open sharing of code via online platforms. The language of Processing is Open Source and users are encouraged to not only engage the framework for design, but also to extend the framework through the development of libraries. Libraries become large pools of unrelated objects that can be accessed by a user in the implementation of a particular design.

Another example is the popular architecture programming framework Grasshopper for Rhino, developed by David Rutten.[20] Grasshopper has popularized parametric design by increasing the accessibility for designers who seek to define networks that can output a multiplicity of outcomes through the simple glide of a slider. It is not the parametric design framework that is of interest here but rather social recombination model that Grasshopper, as well as many other visual programming languages, afford. Grasshopper has been designed to be a discrete combinatorial social tool, where developers are invited to contribute to new self-contained blocks of code in the form of capsules that are later to be recombined by users. The success in adoption of Grasshopper is due to its combinatorial approach to knowledge propagation and not necessarily for the design paradigm (that of parametrics) that it advocates.

From the *Whole Earth Catalog* to Grasshopper, the central structure that precedes social recombination is that of the "list" or repository of objects. Lists are important, as they begin to offer a possible formalization of the Commons. In his book *Alien Phenomenology*, Ian Bogost explores how the format of lists allows breaking from a tradition of continuity;

> Lists offer an antidote to the obsession with Deleuzean becoming, a preference for continuity and smoothness instead of sequentiality and fitfulness.

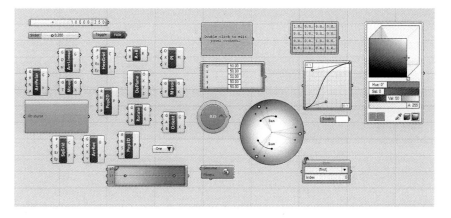

FIGURE 4.1 Grasshopper plug-in for Rhino designed by David Rutten. The programming language is contained in discrete units that can be connected to perform parametric functions. Each unit, following the principles of Object-Oriented Programming, is a self-contained object with inputs and outputs.

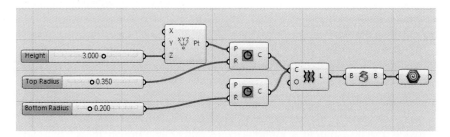

FIGURE 4.2 Grasshopper plug-in for Rhino designed by David Rutten. The connection between units establishes a functional assembly.

The familiar refrain of "becoming-whatever" (it doesn't matter what!) suggests comfort and compatibility in relations between units, thanks to the creative negotiations things make with each other. By contrast, alien phenomenology assumes the opposite: incompatibility. The off-pitch sound of lists to the literary ear only emphasizes their real purpose: disjunction instead of flow. Lists remind us that no matter how fluidly a system may operate, its members nevertheless remain utterly isolated, mutual aliens.[21]

Lists offer a framework for collective construction, one that does not target a cohesive objective or totality like a system but rather targets a field for diverse and even contradictory contributions. Lists offer a framework for formalized Commons, as repositories of discrete units available for recombination. The emergence of value or meaning is linked to the contingent event of design as an act of recombination.

Remixing

Combinatorics or combinatorial design is closely related to the legal battle between copyright lawyers and audiences for the right to remix. Due to the current regulation over intellectual property, any derivative work containing copyrighted material is subject to a penalty.

An important advocate for remixing has been Harvard professor Lawrence Lessig, who has written extensively on the necessity to strengthen our remixing culture and has developed formal protocols for indirect collaboration and sharing through the Creative Commons License. For Lessig, there is a clear distinction between what he calls "Read/Write" culture (RW) and "Read/Only" (RO) culture. RO culture is defined by societies that only consume culture, while RW cultures are able to both consume and produce.[22] This distinction echoes the ideas presented by Jeremy Rifkin and Alvin Toffler when defining a "prosumer" culture, where the consumer becomes the producer of their own goods.[23]

For Lessig, literacy is not just determined by the ability to read but also by the ability to write and potentially alter the content. The current trend of corporate and media development is to develop RO cultures and protect professional creators through copyright laws. The production of consumers are considered amateur and of little value. In an RO culture, the user becomes the resource for the extractive capitalism that was defined in Chapter 1. Read Only means extractivism from rent. This stifles the possibilities for any autonomy or emancipation of the user. On the other hand, a RW culture threatens existing forms of production by providing cheaper alternatives or circumventing production chains, thereby reintroducing the individual's labor into the production process. As Lessig states:

> Yet the history of the Enlightenment is not just the history of teaching kids to read. It is also the history of teaching kids to write. It is the history of literacy—the capacity to understand, which comes not just from passively listening, but also from writing. From the very beginning of human culture,

we have taught our kids RW creativity. We have taught them, that is, how to build upon the culture around us by making reference to that culture or criticizing it ... reading, however, is not enough. Instead, they (or at least the "young people of the day") add to the culture they read by creating and re-creating the culture around them.[24]

What emerges out of Read and Write culture, especially if it is coupled with strong access to Common-Pool Resources and knowledge, is an emancipatory form of DIY culture that is not interested in self-production as a hobby but as a real capacity for organization and participation in and outside the market. If we are to under-stand remixing as a mechanism for social mobility, it is important to dismantle the protectionist provisions that have been achieved by copyright laws that perpetuate a model of value extraction as opposed to value production.

Faced with a socio-political agenda embedded in the notion of remixing, we are to reconsider continuous tectonics that generate, as we have discussed in Chapter 2, impenetrable designs that are resistant to social recomposition. Parametric design, in this sense, contributes to the construction of barriers of entry that annihilate user driven "free innovation."

Combinatorial value production

Through the process of combinatorial design, it is possible to arrive at diverse pos-sible outputs or design patterns. Some of these patterns might prove more valu-able in a given context. The production of (valuable) patterns in a network can be studied by the rate at which an agent exercising recombination is able to explore different information states. For this to happen, a network needs to facilitate ways for order to be accumulated and propagated by the combinatorial actor, who, if we think socially, are the members of a community. This sets in motion a large crowd machine that can explore the possibility space with purpose. MIT physicist Professor César Hidalgo presents a compelling case for the rare configuration of atoms, described as information-rich states defining physical order, writing that "in a physical system, information is the opposite of entropy, as it involves uncommon and highly correlated configurations that are difficult to arrive at."[25] Configurations that are "difficult to arrive at" could be understood in the context of design com-binatorics, as explored in Chapter 3. Discrete units offer less friction to a process of recombination, opening the possibility of a higher number of iterations at the moment of recombination. Moreover, the process of reversibility, an ideal condition for discrete assemblies, allows for a reduction of waste in the form of obsolescence. The role of reversibility for reconfiguration and adaptability as a value proposi-tion can be observed in the notion of "Architecture Mobile" by Yona Friedman (Figure 4.3) or the "Demountable Architecture" of Jean Prouvé (Figure 4.4).

Hidalgo explains how information grows through social structures such as firms. In his studies of the work of economist Ronald Coase, he explains that the friction generated by the cost of interactions, analogous to links in a network, can define the

FIGURE 4.3 Architecture Mobile drawing by Yona Friedman. Architecture is considered as a reversible reconfigurable structure.

system's boundary. Coase uses these properties of links to explain the rise of firms and commercial enterprises. In the words of Hidalgo:

> Coase's intuition tells us that the ability of networks of firms to hold knowledge and know-how will depend on the cost of links. That is, when making and sustaining links is inexpensive, creating large networks of firms will be easier, and accumulating vast volumes of knowledge and know-how will be easier, too. When links are expensive, on the other hand, it will be harder to connect firms, and so it will be harder to create the networks of firms and people needed to accumulate vast volumes of knowledge and know-how. In short, when links are costly, our world becomes fragmented.[26]

This reflection by Hidalgo explains why companies like Apple seek to create autonomous ecosystems for the free exchange of ideas within a company. The closed architecture of Apple demonstrated in the "part-less" design of iPhones are tactics of power asymmetry to consolidate market power and advantage over social production.

A redistribution of power requires a reconsidering of networks as democratic and participatory infrastructures that seek to reduce the cost of links between individuals. A process of social recombination shouldn't be understood as crowd-sourcing, where hierarchy is able to extract value from social contributions but

FIGURE 4.4   6x6 M Demountable House by Jean Prouvé. Prouvé's projects seek to establish protocols of deployment and reversibility, scaling elements to the capacity of human assembly.

Source: Image © Galerie Patrick Seguin.

rather as a flat, peer-to-peer form of mutual aid. Discrete Architecture needs to be understood as an effort to reduce the friction for recombination and increasing the iterative power of social free innovation. In an age of digital communication, the "playground" in which this act of social recombination takes place is the Internet. The project of constructing new standards for digital platforms is an imperative to reclaim the Internet as a tool for the propagation of knowledge and the flow of ideas, and not only as the accumulation of value by network providers.

Democratic platforms

Not all platforms seek to impose a hierarchical and exploitative structure over their users. Author Trebor Scholz has long theorized the impact of digital labor[27] and the possibility of using platforms as collaborative enterprises.[28] Scholz calls this approach "platform cooperativism." Platform cooperativism places value on the ownership of the network and the content being produced, ensuring that the value produced by users to grow a network remains in the hands of users, generating a virtuous cycle. Platform cooperativism attempts to subvert practices of extractivism and exploitation that are commonplace in contemporary hierarchical networks by redefining the operating system of platforms as being aligned with the traditions of cooperative labor practices. As Scholz presents it:

> In opposition to the black-box systems of the Snowden-era Internet, these platforms need to distinguish themselves by making their data flows transparent. Platform co-ops should consider the following principles. The first one, which I explained already, is communal ownership of platforms and protocols. Second, platform co-ops have to be able to offer income security and good pay for all people working for the co-op.[29]

For Scholz, it is not enough to engage in a cooperative business model. He is attempting to reenergize this historic tradition with the power of digital networks, explaining that platforms are the places where we hang out, work and create value. In his studies of platform cooperatives that are already in operation, such as Fairmondo, Stocksy or Coopify, he advocates for the user ownership model of the network, allowing for any profits, commercial or otherwise, to remain in the hands of members.[30]

Current digital platforms operate following the guidelines of a privately owned infrastructure, behaving much like a dictatorship imposing rules and protocols over its users. From social networks to video games, the dictatorial model prevails, not allowing a feedback loop between developers and communities, as the ulterior motives of networks are grounded on the extraction of capital through manipulating behavior. Scholz's proposition can be understood as promoting democracy within digital platforms, where members have rights and can participate in the decisions that dictate how the network operates. Democratic platforms could allow users to vote and actively engage in the protocols that govern the network. Imagine Facebook offering public elections to its users for representatives who will determine which features or privacy policies should be available in the platform. This could allow for collectives to engage in campaigns in favor of data encryption or resisting the commercialization of user data to third parties. This scenario presents a vision of how platforms could open channels of feedback that have been in place in other forms of governance.

Technologies such as peer-to-peer networks or blockchain technology attempt to resolve the asymmetry of power through software architecture. The implementation of distributed systems anticipates the coercive power of centralized networks. Still, stronger regulation and oversight over centralized networks is needed, incentivizing platforms to become more democratic and enforce fair compensation for the value generated by users. The paradigm of user agency defined by a network can drastically change by design, effectively defining what we could call "digital citizenship." The central ethical issues surrounding digital platforms are linked to data collection from users and the rightful ownership of such data. Data authorship and ownership, under the contemporary "Big Data" paradigm, can be traced with fine detail, but it is up to user agreements to establish protocols that are productive and beneficial for both users and platform providers without inheriting asymmetries. Today, Big Data has been extracted through illegitimate means through surveillance strategies. Nevertheless, users celebrate the convenience and performance achieved by data aggregating applications such as Uber or Google. It seems unlikely that we would unroll the series of logistical innovations that have been achieved by Big Data infrastructure, but perhaps we can devise means to legitimize the production and regulate the usage of what ought to be a common and public infrastructure.

In the recent discussions regarding platforms as extractive practices, computer scientist Jaron Lanier has resurfaced the ideas of Internet pioneer Ted Nelson, bringing attention to the value of tracing data's provenance. Lanier attempts to conceptualize a humanistic computing network, one that would care about the prosperity of its members and would not exercise an asymmetric cohesive power over its members. In such a network, every action of every user would be tracked, allowing for a highly granular account of the role of multiple players in any given process. As he explains:

> The foundational idea of humanistic computing is that provenance is valuable. Information is people in disguise, and people ought to be paid for value they contribute that can be sent or stored on a digital network. In humanistic information economics, provenance is treated as a basic right, similar to the way civil rights and property rights were given a universal stature in order to make democracy and market capitalism viable.[31]

Lanier envisions a network that would utilize the two-way links that were proposed by Ted Nelson in the early days of the Internet. For Lanier, a two-way link is fundamental to trace data provenance. Having a two-way cartography could trace the members of a network who contributed to its creation. This could allow a form of micro-payment system to distribute capital to the users.

Within the realm of architectural design, architect and software designer Panagiotis Michalatos has been able to anticipate a transition from file-based sharing to a model where databases store user actions that allow models to be reconstructed from such information.[32] This proposition has profound implications, as it suggests moving away from a model that considers an object or file as output and replaces it with a form of ledger for labor. Users' inputs could define amount to units of value, in which case such value could remain linked to the author who developed it. Lanier has put forward speculative versions of a humanistic network that could generate micro-payments to the creator of value in a network, generating incentives for users to generate and proliferate new content in the hope that over time an accumulation of micro-payments could become something like a pension scheme. As he explains:

> In a humanistic information economy, as people age, they will collect royalties on value they brought into the world when they were younger. This seems to me to be a highly moral use of information technology. It

remembers the right data. The very idea that our world is construed in such a way that the lifetime contributions of hardworking, creative people can be forgotten, that they can be sent perpetually back to the starting gate, is a deep injustice. Putting it that way makes the complaint sound leftist. But today there's also an erasure of what should be legitimate capital. The right should be just as outraged. The proposal here is not redistributionist or socialist. Royalties based on creative contributions from a whole lifetime would always be flowing freshly. It would be wealth earned, not entitlement.[33]

Lanier's proposition has been challenged by authors like Zuboff, who bring to the foreground the unethical objectives behind the accumulation of such data, extracted or paid for. The problem for Zuboff is that behavioral data, the raw material of surveillance capitalism, becomes the instrument for the erosion of democracy through behavior modification. As she laments:

> The remarkable questions here concern the facts that our lives are rendered as behavioral data in the first place; that ignorance is a condition of this ubiquitous rendition; that decision rights vanish before one even knows that there is a decision to make; that there are consequences to this diminishment of rights that we can neither see nor foretell; that there is no exit, no voice, and no loyalty, only helplessness, resignation, and psychic numbing; and that encryption is the only positive action left to discuss when we sit around the dinner table and casually ponder how to hide from the forces that hide from us.[34]

Like Assange, Zuboff evokes the need for instruments such as encryption to regulate the illegitimate extraction of user data. The question that emerges is whether there are design protocols to ensure the production of common repositories of data that can serve in the production of prosperity as a public infrastructure while regulating the practice of behavioral modification.

Independent of the software architecture that allows or enforces the production and distribution of value, there is still the issue of allowing for platforms to remain open for alterations. A closed system will always treat the public as users, bound to operate into a predefined playing field.

Playbor

Social activity performed on digital platforms not only equates to correlational data that might be used for learning algorithms but can also blur the lines between social activity and labor. By gamifying tedious tasks, digital platforms are able to engage audiences into working without compensation. What has come to be known as crowdsourcing is the practice of externalizing labor costs of a company to a crowd that will perform it for free. The term "playbor" has been utilized to denominate the blurring between "play" and "labor," denouncing an exploitative practice of corporations to cutting costs by outsourcing their production to a user.[35]

While a platform can utilize crowd engagement to solve problems or perform repetitive tasks such as the Amazon Mechanical Turk, where small repetitive and laborious tasks are distributed over a large population of cloud workers, other initiatives use the coordination of crowds to solve large, and often socially sensitive, issues. Developed at the University of Washington, the video game *Foldit* (Figure 4.5) attempted to offer a protein-folding simulation game that could be used to solve protein-folding puzzles. These three-dimensional structures had been historically difficult for algorithms to address. The *Foldit* proposition relied on the power of players to socialize the process. A player could slowly learn by solving simple puzzles, slowly developing the expertise toward proteins that had not been solved by scientists yet. The players were not alone, as an online community quickly grew around the project, where players would share tips and recipes with one another. It was this communication between members of a crowd that allowed for solution of players that provided breakthroughs in science. As was presented in the team's paper in the journal *Nature*:

> As interesting as the Foldit predictions themselves is the complexity, variation and creativity of the human search process. Foldit gameplay supports both competition and collaboration between players. For collaboration, players can share structures with their group members, and help each other out with strategies and tips through the game's chat function, or across the wiki. The competition and collaboration create a large social aspect to the game, which alters the aggregate search progress of Foldit and heightens player motivation.

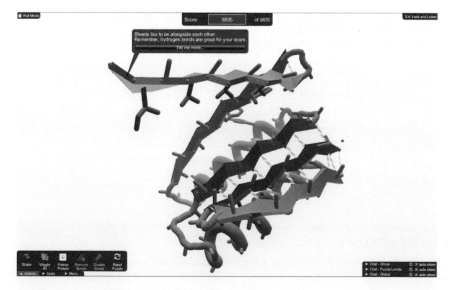

FIGURE 4.5   *Foldit* Video Game by University of Washington Center for Game Science. The game allows players to contribute to scientific discovery by solving protein-folding puzzles within a video game environment.

> As groups compete for higher rankings and discover new structures, other
> groups appear to be motivated to play more, and within groups the exchange
> of solutions can help other members catch up to the leaders.[36]

The game is a simulation engine, working together with wikis and forums to constitute a powerful infrastructure for coordination and communication between
players. But games such as *Foldit* face the difficult decision between becoming
protocols of value extraction, where the labor of users could be harvested for the
benefit of research sponsors, or defining protocols for the production of Commons,
where knowledge generated by users could remain as part of the public domain.

A critical challenge in an age of inequality is to conceive of mechanisms where
the power of social platforms is put toward the service of common goals, and not,
as argued by Italian economist Christian Marazzi, as a mechanism for companies to
externalize labor to consumers thereby reducing their own internal costs. The latter
result is a consumer who is complicit in the production of value for a company. As
Marazzi explains:

> Empirical examples of the externalization of value production, of its exten-
> sion into the sphere of circulation, are now abundant. Ever since the first
> phase of company outsourcing (subcontractors to suppliers and external con-
> sultants), which, beginning with the 1980s, saw the emergence of atypical
> labor and second generation autonomous labor (freelance, entrepreneurs of
> themselves, former employees that became self-employed) along the lines of
> the "Toyota Model," capitalist colonization of the circulation sphere has been
> nonstop, to the point of transforming the consumer into a veritable producer
> of economic value. Co-production, where the individual is the co-producer
> of what he consumes, "is today at the heart of the strategies of public and
> private companies. They put the consumer to work in various phases of the
> value creation."[37]

An alternative to the dynamics observed by Marazzi can occur if social production
by citizens facilitated by digital networks generates value that remains in the hands
of users or the communities to which they belong. The framework of Platform
Cooperativism proposed by Scholz relies on social production in the age of the
Internet but focuses on the final beneficiary of the value produced in order to
legitimize the commercialization of leisure.

Combinatorial design as a culture of remixing may prove to be a scalable model
for the production of goods and services, especially if it manages to be implemented
at the scale of digital platforms. The asymmetry between the network and the
consumer has grown out of proportion, requiring further architectures to restore
rights and redefine the ethics of privacy. Digital applications and video games can
be conceptualized as technologies for the production of the Commons, where data
and value do not end up in hands of platform providers but rather in the public
domain, enabling further proliferation of value through processes of recombination.

In cases where labor and social production are not a search function over a clearly pre-defined domain with possible optimal solutions but a cultural domain where value is not discovered but contingently created out of social codes and interactions, users should receive full governance for their contributions and a legal mechanism in order to claim ownership. The argument that has been put forward stands behind user ownership of production, protected by encryption and regulation. The attempt is to reduce the capacity of platforms to extract behavioral data, underscoring their role as public infrastructure managers.

Architectural platforms

The conceptualization of a platform presents the same challenges and opportunities for architecture as it does for other industries. Platforms democratize the design process, advancing the tools and literacy of a crowd by establishing knowledge propagation channels. By socializing design, users are able to build larger databases of references that will aid in solutions for new projects. Patterns can emerge, offering standard solutions for re-occurring cases. The crowd will also develop design literacy, as what is sophisticated will be rare and scarce, demonstrating the effort necessary for achieving quality. On the other end of the spectrum, all design production could end up belonging to a private network, orchestrating the free labor of crowds for knowledge production, one that could feed artificial intelligence algorithms. The current competition model, a dominant model for value extraction in architecture, could be accelerated to a far wider form of digital labor extraction.

It has become urgent for the field of architecture to engage in the conceptualization and design of platform infrastructure, offering core values and denouncing practices of exploitation. To do so, research in architectural technology associated with the development of tools needs to venture outside established solutions offered by the industry. Platform research should have the main objective of engaging with a social system and looking into technologies and communities that have already started exhibiting interest in participation and the proliferation of knowledge and content within a network. As has been argued by Professor Yochai Benkler, it is possible to design networks biased for cooperation. He states that ingredients like "communication," "authenticity," "empathy," "solidarity" and the construction of "moral systems"[38] are the most challenging and key attributes to be embedded in the design of digital platforms that can allow for breakthroughs in social cooperation.

Video games are an interactive medium where players are able to engage with the production of form and systems thinking. They have shown great potential to advance an architectural agenda that attempts to democratize access to local fabrication and community development. Games such as *Minecraft* that have a network of nearly 75 million players have the closest resemblance to what we could consider a social platform for spatial content. Games have been able to establish a two-way dialogue between users and developers, actively participating in the production of a network via forums, polls and streams among other forms of digital

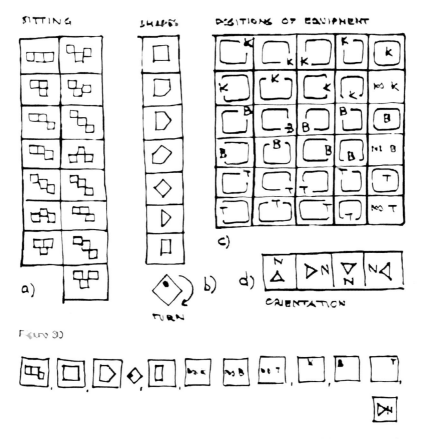

FIGURE 4.6 Flatwriter, 1967, was a computer program conceived by Yona Friedman to enable the user to design the plan of his future home (self-planning) in the Ville Spatiale, or for a citizen to redesign his neighborhood in the Ville Spatiale.

content. Games have also adopted a practice of modding, where a platform opens channels for user modification, although such practices have been studied as forms of exploitative labor.[39] Nevertheless, game environments have been able to develop a medium conducive for combinatorial design, as with games such as *Minecraft* (Figure 4.7) or *Cities Skylines* (Figure 4.8), and knowledge of how to embed robust educational protocols as is exhibited in innumerable in-game tutorials that lead players to advance game states. All these attributes position game environments as strong candidates for the development of architectural platforms. The medium of games has matured over time, allowing for close approximations of reality, as is the case with games such as *Kerbal Space Program*, which has been embraced by NASA for expanding the literacy of the challenges of the agency.[40] In recent initiatives, figures like Lawrence Lessig have started developing projects that could be able to simulate and tinker with models of governance. For example, the Seed project

FIGURE 4.7   Block by Block initiative by UN-Habitat using *Minecraft* video game to rebuild and envision real-world development.

FIGURE 4.8   *Cities Skyline* video game by Colossal Order. Urban city simulation.

proposes a simulation game where players are required to design and manage the economy of an exo-planet.[41] For Lessig, the challenge is not to iterate over expertly conceived design to arrive at a model that works but rather to sit back and allow for thousands of simulated economies to be created and managed from the bottom up, allowing for the study of stable patterns that emerge.[42]

While we could consider architectural platforms as repositories of already created content as is the case with 3DWarehouse[43] or as a private dashboard for team coordination as in the case with Modelo.io.,[44] games have managed to socialize the design process, allowing for multiple participants to interact with one another directly and indirectly through the sharing of digital content.

Projects such as *Block'hood* (Figure 4.9 and 4.10) and *Common'hood* (Figure 4.11 and 4.12) are video games that attempt to allow users to design and explore

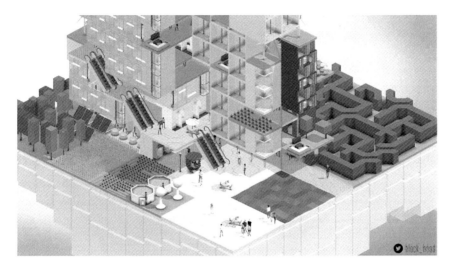

FIGURE 4.9   *Block'hood* video game by Jose Sanchez, Plethora Project. Urban simulation based on ecology and interdependence of inhabitants. Educational platform.

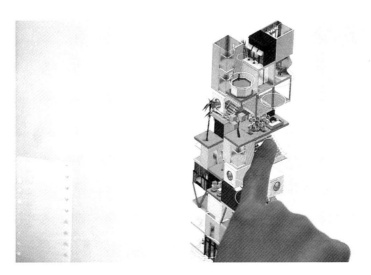

FIGURE 4.10   *Block'hood* video game by Jose Sanchez, Plethora Project. The game has been used as a tool for social participation developing literacy on ecological systems.

FIGURES 4.11 AND 4.12 *Common'hood* video game by Jose Sanchez, Plethora Project. Fabrication and design video game mediated by economic scarcity and social struggle. The game is a platform to aid self-provisioning of architecture.

socioeconomical problems associated with their local communities. Platforms are utilized as a dashboard for combinatorial design aiming for the production of literacy and the development of digital infrastructure for participation and self-provisioning. At the core of these initiatives is an interest in generating architectural principles and designs that engage the world through a scope of resource management, systems thinking and ecological interdependence. The challenge is to effectively create a platform that is aimed at the construction of the common knowledges and repositories of architecture alternatives.

For architecture, platforms offer an opportunity to populate the landscape between experts and non-experts, generating a spectrum that could both appreciate and actively participate in the production of cultural value, operating as designers, curators or community managers. The expansion of the discipline toward user-created content does not threaten the discipline with a form of deprofessionalization. On the contrary, it suggests a much larger portion of our population could take part in a critical discourse of citizenship through participation. The opportunity for "free innovation" as framed by von Hippel acts as a form of autonomous practice, especially for those communities that have lost access to capital and are able to use labor and knowledge as a mechanism to defeat debt. For these scenarios to take place, we need to design platforms that allow user collaboration and participation while maintaining the value produced in the hands of users. This incentivizes the knowledge that is contributed to common pool repositories that can remain in the public domain. If such ethical imperatives are to be realized by experimental platform design, they can become examples and even expected standards for already established competitors, allowing the crowds to enforce them by popular demand.

Notes

1 Nick Srnicek, *Platform Capitalism* (Polity, 2017).
2 Srnicek, *Platform Capitalism.*
3 Tiziana Terranova, *Network Culture: Politics for the Information Age* (Pluto Press, 2004).
4 Srnicek, *Platform Capitalism.*
5 Shoshana Zuboff, *The Age of Surveillance Capitalism: The Fight for a Human Future at the New Frontier of Power* (PublicAffairs, 2019).
6 Zuboff, *The Age of Surveillance Capitalism.*
7 Matthew Rosenberg, Nicholas Confessore, and Carole Cadwalladr, 'How Trump Consultants Exploited the Facebook Data of Millions,' *The New York Times*, 2018 <www.nytimes.com/2018/04/12/technology/mark-zuckerberg-testimony.html>. [accessed 3 November 2018].
8 Julian Assange and Others, *Cypherpunks: Freedom and the Future of the Internet* (OR Books, 2016).
9 Assange and Others, *Cypherpunks.*
10 Zuboff, *The Age of Surveillance Capitalism.*
11 Stewart Brand, *The Whole Earth Catalog* (Random House, 1971).
12 Richard Stallman, 'Free Software, Freedom and Cooperation,' 2001 <www.gnu.org/events/rms-nyu-2001-transcript.txt> [accessed 16 June 2014].
13 Joseph E. Stiglitz, *People, Power, and Profits: Progressive Capitalism for an Age of Discontent* (W.W. Norton & Company, 2019).
14 David Bollier, *Think Like a Commoner: A Short Introduction to the Life of the Commons* (New Society Publishers, 2014).
15 Stiglitz, *People, Power, and Profits.*
16 Stiglitz, *People, Power, and Profits.*
17 Eric Von Hippel, *Free Innovation* (MIT Press, 2016).
18 Von Hippel, *Free Innovation.*
19 Casey Reas and Ben Fry, 'Processing,' 2001 <https://processing.org/> [accessed 10 October 2015].
20 David Rutten, 'Grasshopper Interface Explained,' 2015 <https://wiki.mcneel.com/labs/explicithistory/interfaceexplained>. [accessed 6 June 2018].

21 Ian Bogost, *Alien Phenomenology, Or What It's Like to Be a Thing* (University of Minnesota Press, 2012).

22 Lawrence Lessig, *Remix: Making Art and Commerce Thrive in the Hybrid Economy* (Penguin Books, 2008).

23 Jeremy Rifkin, *The Zero Marginal Cost Society* (Palgrave Macmillan, 2014).

24 Lessig, *Remix.*

25 Cesar Hidalgo, *Why Information Grows: The Evolution of Order, from Atoms to Economies,* First edit (Basic Books, 2015).

26 Hidalgo, *Why Information Grows.*

27 Trebor Scholz, *Digital Labor: The Internet as Playground and Factory* (Routledge, 2013).

28 Trebor Scholz and Nathan Schneide, *Ours to Hack and to Own: The Rise of Platform Cooperativism, a New Vision for the Future of Work and a Fairer Internet* (OR Books, 2016).

29 Scholz and Schneide, *Ours to Hack and to Own.*

30 Scholz and Schneide, *Ours to Hack and to Own.*

31 Jaron Lanier, *Who Owns the Future?* (Simon & Schuster, 2013).

32 Michalatos Panagiotis, 'Design Signals,' in *Digital Property: Open-Source Architecture (Architectural Design),* ed. by Wendy W. Fok and Antoine Picon (Academy Press, 2016).

33 Lanier, *Who Own the Future.*

34 Zuboff, *The Age of Surveillance Capitalism.*

35 Julian Kücklich, 'Precarious Playbour: Modders and the Digital Games Industry,' *The Fiberculture Journal* (5) (2005) <http://five.fibreculturejournal.org/fcj-025-precarious-playbour-modders-and-the-digital-games-industry/>.

36 Seth Cooper and Association for Computing Machinery, *A Framework for Scientific Discovery through Video Games* (Morgan & Claypool Publishers, 2014).

37 Christian Marazzi, *The Violence of Financial Capitalism* (Semiotext(e), 2011).

38 Yochai Benkler, *The Penguin and the Leviathan: How Cooperation Triumphs Over Self-Interest* (Crown Business, 2011).

39 Kücklich, 'Precarious Playbour.'

40 Sam White, 'Minecraft in Space: Why Nasa Is Embracing Kerbal Space Program,' *The Guardian,* 2014 <www.theguardian.com/technology/2014/may/22/kerbal-space-program-why-nasa-minecraft> [accessed 7 June 2018].

41 Klang Games, Lawrence Lessig, 'Seed,' 2017 <https://seed-project.io/>.

42 Jordan Pearson, '"Governance in the Real World Is So Fucked": Lawrence Lessig Is Working on an MMO,' *Motherboard,* 2017 <https://motherboard.vice.com/en_us/article/neweqm/lawrence-lessig-is-working-on-an-mmo-game-seed>. [accessed 11 November 2018].

43 Trimble, *3D Warehouse.* < https://3dwarehouse.sketchup.com/> [accessed 12 November 2019].

44 Qi Su and Tian Deng, *Modelo,'* (2017). https://modelo.io/ [accessed 12 November 2019].

References

Assange, Julian, Jacob Appelbaum, Andy Muller-Maguhn, and Jérémie Zimmermann, *Cypherpunks: Freedom and the Future of the Internet* (OR Books, New York, London, 2012–2016)

Benkler, Yochai, *The Penguin and the Leviathan: How Cooperation Triumphs Over Self-Interest* (Crown Business, New York, 2011)

Bogost, Ian, *Alien Phenomenology, Or What It's Like to Be a Thing* (University of Minnesota Press, Minneapolis, 2012)

Bollier, David, *Think Like a Commoner: A Short Introduction to the Life of the Commons* (New Society Publishers, Gabriola Island, 2014)

Brand, Stewart, *The Whole Earth Catalog* (Random House, 1971)

Cooper, Seth, and Association for Computing Machinery, *A Framework for Scientific Discovery through Video Games* (Morgan & Claypool Publishers, 2014)

Hidalgo, Cesar, *Why Information Grows: The Evolution of Order, from Atoms to Economies*, First edit (Basic Books, New York, 2015)

Trimble, *3D Warehouse* <https://3dwarehouse.sketchup.com/> [accessed 12 November 2019]

Kücklich, Julian, 'Precarious Playbour: Modders and the Digital Games Industry,' *The Fiberculture Journal* (5) (2005) <http://five.fibreculturejournal.org/fcj-025-precarious-playbour-modders-and-the-digital-games-industry/> [accessed 03 March 2018]

Lanier, Jaron, *Who Own the Future* (Simon & Schuster, New York, 2013)

Lessig, Lawrence, *Remix: Making Art and Commerce Thrive in the Hybrid Economy* (Penguin Books, New York, 2008)

———, 'Seed,' Klang Games 2017–2020 <https://seed-project.io/> [accessed 20 November 2018]

Marazzi, Christian, *The Violence of Financial Capitalism* (Semiotext(e), Los Angeles, 2011)

Michalatos, Panagiotis, 'Design Signals,' in *Digital Property: Open-Source Architecture (Architectural Design)*, ed. by Wendy W. Fok and Antoine Picon (John Wiley & Sons, Oxford, 2016)

Pearson, Jordan, '"Governance in the Real World Is So Fucked": Lawrence Lessig Is Working on an MMO,' *Motherboard*, 2017 <https://motherboard.vice.com/en_us/article/neweqm/lawrence-lessig-is-working-on-an-mmo-game-seed> [accessed 11 November 2018]

Reas, Casey, and Ben Fry, 'Processing,' 2001 <https://processing.org/> [accessed 10 October 2015]

Rifkin, Jeremy, *The Zero Marginal Cost Society* (Palgrave Macmillan, New York, 2014)

Rosenberg, Matthew, Nicholas Confessore, and Carole Cadwalladr, 'How Trump Consultants Exploited the Facebook Data of Millions,' *The New York Times*, 2018 <www.nytimes.com/2018/04/12/technology/mark-zuckerberg-testimony.html> [accessed 3 November 2018]

Rutten, David, 'Grasshopper Interface Explained,' 2015 <https://wiki.mcneel.com/labs/explicithistory/interfaceexplained> [accessed 6 June 2018]

Scholz, Trebor, *Digital Labor: The Internet as Playground and Factory* (Routledge, Abingdon, 2013)

———, 'How Platform Cooperativism Can Unleash the Network,' *Re:Publica*, 2016 <www.youtube.com/watch?v=bkSTgAucRqE> [accessed 11 October 2018]

Scholz, Trebor, and Nathan Schneide, *Ours to Hack and to Own: The Rise of Platform Cooperativism, a New Vision for the Future of Work and a Fairer Internet* (OR Books, New York and London, 2016)

Srnicek, Nick, *Platform Capitalism* (Polity Press, Cambridge, 2017)

Stallman, Richard, 'Free Software, Freedom and Cooperation,' 2001 <www.gnu.org/events/rms-nyu-2001-transcript.txt> [accessed 16 June 2014]

Stiglitz, Joseph E., *People, Power, and Profits: Progressive Capitalism for an Age of Discontent* (W. W. Norton & Company, New York, 2019)

Su, Qi, and Tian Deng, *Modelo*,' (2017) <https://modelo.io/> [accessed 12 November 2018]

Terranova, Tiziana, *Network Culture: Politics for the Information Age* (Pluto Press, London and Ann Arbor, 2004)

Von Hippel, Eric, *Free Innovation* (MIT Press, Cambridge, 2016)

White, Sam, 'Minecraft in Space: Why Nasa Is Embracing Kerbal Space Program,' *The Guardian*, 2014 <www.theguardian.com/technology/2014/may/22/kerbal-space-program-why-nasa-minecraft> [accessed 7 June 2018]

Zuboff, Shoshana, *The Age of Surveillance Capitalism: The Fight for a Human Future at the New Frontier of Power* (PublicAffairs, New York, 2019)

5

RECONSTRUCTION THROUGH SELF-PROVISION

From shared value to the Commons

In 2011 economist Michael Porter put forward the idea of "shared value" as a way for corporations to reconnect economic success with social progress. He states that capitalism is perceived to generate profit at the expense of communities and that this is due to an outdated view of the creation of value, one that focuses on short-term gains and exploitative practices. By shared value, Porter is not suggesting increasing social responsibility of corporations or augmenting peripheral programs like sustainability or philanthropy. On the contrary, he calls for the reshaping of core practices of corporations toward long-term alignment of economic value with societal value.

The key idea behind the creation of shared value is an understanding of the value chain and the recognition of societal needs that enable that value chain to remain healthy and generate benefits to all participants. Porter explains that an externality such as pollution is recast as a shared value concern for a corporation's understanding of the well-being of the value chain and the sustaining of a long-term commitment to the communities it serves. To explain this, Porter uses the example of fair-trade, explaining that it does not necessarily increase productivity but rather only offers a redistribution. His vision of shared value seeks to empower local producers with education and new technologies, allowing them not only to increase their revenue substantially but also to increase the overall productivity of the chain. He presents the example of Côte d'Ivoire, where fair trade could increase income by 10% to 20% and shared value investments can raise income by more than 300%.[1]

This is certainly a step in the right direction. As a result, there may be the temptation to equate the idea of shared value to the reconstruction of the Commons. This would be a mistake, as underlying the idea of shared value is a production chain where individuals fulfill fixed roles. The value of Porter's proposition is the break-ing of a zero-sum game mentality where corporate growth is at odds with social progress. His proposition does not intend to provide any emancipatory powers or social mobility to members in the value chain. Neither does it attempt to recover cultural heritage that has been erased by practices of extractivism, exploitation and subjugation. It is from these values that we can identify that the Commons needs to operate as an autonomous scaffold for the production of commonwealth by embracing non-market logic and allowing social mobility and indeterminacy. The production of such a scaffold needs to be the outcome of social production, forms of cooperation that yield new opportunities for others, if it is to develop a sense of value and purpose. This presents an organizational challenge, as traditional forms of hierarchical control fail to allow for the function of value to remain open-ended. This means that the only measure of progress is through the growth of indicators such as GDP. Attempts to develop movements for the liberation of knowledge (such as the protests in support of net neutrality in 2012, environmental activists such as Extinction Rebellion addressing the imperative of combating climate change or movements that have emerged as a response of economic inequality, such as Occupy Wall Street in 2011 and the uprising in Chile in 2019) have found strong opposition, demonstrating the momentum of the current economic model and the lack of will, especially for those who are now in power, to make any changes.

The inevitable social transformations occurring should not only lead toward a redistribution of wealth or regulation of carbon emissions but should also consider the design and construction of a social infrastructure defined as the Commons.

Commons as potential

During the 2012 Venice Architectural Biennale, the architect Pier Vittorio Aureli put forward an understanding of the Common in architecture that would go beyond the historical definition of the Commons as Common-Pool Resources (CPR). He asserted that the Common is defined by all material and immaterial architectural projects that contribute to the discipline of architecture. To make his argument, Aureli utilizes Paolo Virno's distinction between potentiality and actual-ity. As he explained, "Potentiality is the infinite range of possibilities not yet deter-mined into finite things, the historically determined reality of the possible. Actuality is the determination of what is potential in the form of finite things and events."[2] Like Virno, Aureli emphasizes the inability of the actual to exhaust the range of possibilities offered by the potential. The Common is in fact understood as the mechanism that allows the potential.

> To make the common explicit means to theorize architecture not as a prod-uct of individual contributions, but as a collective force, a pre-individual reality that is both the productive basis of architectural production but also

something autonomous, something that exceeds its technical and commercial determinations and which addresses and manifests our collective understanding of the space in which we live.[3]

Contemporary digital platforms are also playgrounds that operate under the notion of potentiality and actuality. In a digital platform a user is placed into a constructed domain, operating under the illusion of freedom. The domain of the platform dictates what is possible but has been heavily pre-designed to limit the range of action and, as we have discussed in Chapter 4, leads to the production of behavioral assets and the possibility of behavior modification in its users. In a platform, a user operates within a system of expectation where most actions follow a predictable pattern. This predictable behavior, returning to Taleb's denomination, is understood as a "White Swan,"[4] a highly predictable event. The behavior or actions of a user define a form of actualization that can be forecasted and lives within a space of a behavioral prediction. It is possible that a user generates unexpected behavior, what Taleb calls a "Black Swan," that alters our understanding of the domain. Such pattern of behavior resides in the blind spot of a system of expectation.

Aureli's definition of the Commons still retains Elinor Ostrom's framework for understanding the Common as a CPR or commonwealth. In his case, these resources also include a wider notion of immaterial resources such as information and knowledge. However, we are yet to understand the role of Commons as social systems of organization and governance that are able not only to operate within a pre-established domain, as in the case of shared value, but also capable of constructing and altering the underlying established framework of production. The introduction of digital platforms, as discussed previously, presents a double-edged sword, as on the one hand it can greatly limit the democratic rights of users, and on the other, offers an environment for combinatorial surplus, where it is possible to construct Commons as welfare infrastructure allowing for education, organization and production.

Architect Alastair Parvin has argued that it is necessary to "design down the threshold" for design production.[5] This reduction of the barrier of entry established a first principle to challenge the market power that has been obtained through vertical integration. Reducing the barrier of entry means an opposition to market systems and design paradigms that only seek to maximize capital extraction through rent seeking practices and the exploitation of labor. "Designing down the threshold" declares awareness of the unsustainable inequality implicit in the current economic model and offers design a framework for participating and contributing to the construction of an alternative that does not only operate as a sink for capital. Zuboff has argued that the surveillance capitalist agenda that has been imposed over technological development is not intrinsic to technology[6] but is a design decision that has evolved out of an underregulated market. Therefore, the production of a value system that positions the Commons as a central urgent effort to rebalance market asymmetries will come with its own form of architecture, tectonics and tools for social coordination.

Breaking the domain

Digital platforms have progressively advanced the regulation of users on the Internet. The battle for personal freedoms on the Internet has been fought by activists since the first attempts to establish the United States Combating Online Infringement and Counterfeits Act (COICA) in 2010. COICA was a precursor to what later became the Preventing Real Online Threats to Economic Creativity and Theft of Intellectual Property Act (PIPA) and the Stop Online Piracy Act (SOPA). These bills sought to allow Internet Service Providers (ISPs) to shut down or limit access to websites deemed to be "dedicated to infringement activities."[7] As has been presented by David Moon in his documentation of the organized efforts to stop SOPA:

> SOPA's provisions were thought to cover platforms for user-generated content—even if the platform's owners harbored no intent to host infringing material, and even if they were unaware of said content. It was ostensibly targeted at foreign sites—bad enough in its own right—but COICA's proponents had also targeted the domestic web, making clear their ultimate designs. Many feared that under SOPA domestic sites like search engines or social media platforms that merely linked to targeted foreign sites could also be penalized.[8]

SOPA has been described as an attack on net neutrality. Fundamentally, an attack on net neutrality is an attack on the Commons, in terms of the way in which knowledge is accessed, constructed and disseminated. The romanticized idea that all of our disciplinary knowledge defines a public Common that is constantly becoming a driving force for new knowledge is destroyed by formal attempts such as SOPA to legally limit such access and protect forms of intellectual property and practices of monetization from public knowledge. As we have discussed, intellectual property and copyright are rent-seeking mechanisms that operate as value extraction rather than value production.

An activist who understood the implications behind PIPA and SOPA was Aaron Swartz. From an early age Swartz participated in the construction of the Internet's infrastructure. He contributed to the development of the RSS protocol when he was a young teenager and contributed to the development of the Creative Commons. His politics have been linked to allowing the Internet to become a tool for access, dedicating most of his work to designing mechanisms of access to common knowledge. In 2008 Swartz decided to work on a project that would allow public access to federal court data in the United States. This data was kept in a system called Pacer. Swartz adapted a scraping algorithm to automate the downloading of Pacer documents from free access computers that were installed in public libraries.[9] This placed Swartz under the eye of the FBI.[10] In time, Swartz became more interested in the idea of further "freeing" public knowledge and he started looking at journal gatekeeping companies such as Elsevier and JSTOR. Swartz couldn't comprehend how the accumulation of scientific public knowledge stored in journal publications like JSTOR were behind expensive subscription protocols that ultimately restricted access to this information. Swartz was later caught running a scraping operation of his network access at MIT. He was downloading a large number of articles from the JSTOR catalog. Prosecutors utilized his writing, in particular his "Open Guerrilla Access Manifesto," to make the case that Swartz was attempting to fully download the JSTOR catalog with the intention to sharing it in the public domain. This is an excerpt from Swartz's "Open Guerrilla Access Manifesto":

> Information is power. But like all power, there are those who want to keep it for themselves. The world's entire scientific and cultural heritage, published over centuries in books and journals, is increasingly being digitized and locked up by a handful of private corporations. Want to read the papers featuring the most famous results of the sciences? You'll need to send enormous amounts to publishers like Reed Elsevier.[11]

Swartz actions break from the standard predictable behavior of a user. His transgressions aimed to reclaim the space of potentiality granted by the Common that had been victim of market enclosures. He utilized his access and knowledge to redefine the domain that citizens could operate in, one that was progressively shrinking due to the implementation of gatekeeping technologies. He was prosecuted by the Secret Service's Electronic Crimes Working Group, which sought to make an example out of Swartz's case. He was indicted on federal felony charges and was facing more than 50 years in federal prison when he took his own life at the age of 26.

Swartz wasn't operating within a system of expectations such as Taleb's White Swan, nor was he operating as a virtuoso player who would reveal patterns rare to come by such as Taleb's Black Swan. He was an expert who was aware that the domain of possibilities was larger than what was being presented to the public. He was an agent who sought to redefine the space of potentiality. Swartz's actions do not belong to the expectation of the network and could not be forecasted or predicted, therefore they were rendered illegal. Swartz understood that it is not enough to play between White and Black Swans. His actions echo Elie Ayache's criticism targeting the system of provision and expectation:[12] the fixed, regulated domain. Swartz's actions operate as "Blank Swans" and fundamentally defend the attack on the Commons, resisting the shrinking of personal freedoms in the public realm of the Internet. Swartz's actions seem to be aware of Aureli's notion of the Common, as a pre-individual reality that antecedes any personal contribution, an action that is not yet tabulated into a domain.[13]

Swartz as an activist and hacker aimed to defend the pre-individual freedoms that had been colonized by digital networks, hoping for new avenues for self-provision. Under this critical lens of possible actions of users within a pre-established domain, Swartz demonstrated the capacity of users to dynamically alter the domain that they operate in, as they are the source of value and meaning emerging from a network.

Allowing users to alter and redefine the domain of platforms is highly inefficient for commercial network providers, as it suggests breaking the protocol of user standardization that has been put in place by platforms. Yet the possibility of altering the rules of the playing field through popular consensus is what is called democracy. What is necessary for technology today is not only its democratization but more importantly, the bringing of democracy into technology. The illusion of "open platforms" that is presented in the forms of plug-ins, add-ons or mods that are developed by third parties to expand the functionality of a software does not permeate the authoritative governance residing in the hierarchy of the network. None of these modes of contribution challenge the standardization of users being implemented by platforms, nor do they contribute to the embedding of democratic values into networks. These contributions only aggregate and legitimize the building of predictable domains for users.

The role of Open Source

The actions of Aaron Swartz were argued to operate outside the law, demonstrating that there is no avenue within the domain of the network to challenge or address inefficiencies and user concerns regarding privacy and freedoms. The current legal system, as demonstrated with the Swartz case, guarantees that platforms manage and constrain the actions of users, hindering the space of potentiality of the Commons. This gives evidence of how digital platforms have become factories for the standardization and tabulation of behavior, not the enablers that they claim to be. The advocacy for protocols of production such as Open Source or Creative Commons practices precede the regulatory role of platforms. Open Source plays a role of transparency and ability for oversight as well as offering the capacity to break or expand a technological domain. Open Source antecedes the needs for Swartz's actions, embedding into the technology the mechanisms for their potential alteration.

Architects Carlo Ratti and Matthew Claudel's definition of Open Source architecture centers around current understandings of projects like Wikipedia and Linux[14] and how the ethos of such initiatives have been carried toward manufacturing and fabrication with initiatives such as the Fablabs at MIT by Professor Neil Gershenfeld. Ratti and Claudel also utilize Open Source examples such as the Arduino project in order to suggest a progressive shift toward cooperative design. In their model for Open Source architecture, many contributors use a versioning control software to gradually evolve designs by making small contributions, thus dissolving traditional ideas of authorship.[15] Still, theorists such as Evgeny Morozov have echoed studies that question the unquestioned role of openness. Morozov refers to studies performed by UCLA anthropologist Chris Kelty, who questions the merit of openness, asking if openness is a goal in itself or a means to achieving something else, and if so, what?[16] Morozov argues that the Internet has been dominated by an "openness fundamentalism, where openness is seen as a fail-safe solution to virtually any problem."[17] Morozov calls for a critical evaluation on "how openness may be fostering or harming innovation, promoting or demoting justice, facilitating or complicating deliberation."[18]

Morozov refers to how the idea of openness has been hijacked by the architects of the current Internet, such as Google, to portray an image of openness,[19] while the opposite is true, as has been demonstrated by the studies of Zuboff.[20] Still, the idea of openness, linked to an Open Source of networks in the context of Aaron Swartz's actions, is linked to the protection of democracy. Swartz's actions operate as a whistle-blower who, having the technical knowledge, understands the power of networks for eroding democratic rights.

Open Source plays an important role in the development of transparent and cooperative platforms and the design of public infrastructure. Yet while Open Source frameworks construct a democratic scaffold at the core of its technological infrastructure, Open Source also trends toward collaboration between expert users. There is an important distinction between the source code and the documentation or the development of educational infrastructure to disseminate such knowledge. This was pointed out by Swartz in an interview when he was a teenager. When asked about the lack of intuitive user interfaces (UI) in Open Source software, he said:

> Well, for most of these programmers UI is hard, because they don't understand it. They see things textually, not visually. The free software culture comes very much from the Unix culture, and Unix is very much expert-oriented. Experts don't need "good UI"—they know exactly what to do already and they just want to be able to do it as fast as they can. This is related to the other problem, which is that free software programmers code mostly for themselves. And since they completely and intuitively understand the software, it doesn't seem like the UI is bad to them—to them, it makes perfect sense.[21]

This perspective allows us to separate the production of Open Source content from the production of documentation or accessibility resources. The term Open Source, associated with the idea of open access, ensures the former, not the latter. Some programmers are very good at producing documentation and learning resources but some are very bad. Many Open Source projects have literacy barriers, and do not achieve a central concern of reducing the barrier of entry or potential alteration of established infrastructure.

The example of the Processing software created by Casey Reas and Ben Fry[22] and the community surrounding it can be studied to understand the importance of documentation and the production of learning paths. Processing is a free Open Source software that offers a simplified Java programming interface. The project is an Open Source effort to "design down the threshold" of programming. This is achieved because of a large number of examples and their documentation provided by the Processing Foundation and the community that creates a "literacy ladder" for Processing. This ladder is defined by how the spectrum of knowledge is populated between new, inexperienced users and experts.

In a project for the construction or fortification of the Commons, Open Source plays an important role, not because there is a goal in openness, but rather as a form of scrutiny of the digital platforms that exercise algorithmic governance. In this sense, production of the Commons defines a larger umbrella of goals, where Open Source could be discussed as one of the technical protocols of implementation. Alternatives are also welcome, as Open Source should not become a fixed truism, but rather one of the avenues for embedding democracy in technology and ensuring mechanisms for scrutiny and regulation.

The literacy ladder

A call for the reconstruction of the Commons is to acknowledge the social structures and contributions that are necessary to populate the literacy ladder in the public domain. The literacy ladder is a form of social production where participants of a network are able to populate a spectrum of knowledge. A weak ladder might take the form of an Open Source project that has been developed among expert users with very little documentation for how to engage and access such knowledge. The strong literacy ladder, on the other hand, is a road map to knowledge that emphasizes a gradual upward mobility. While this is a process well known to educators, as educational programs are designed in the form of degrees, many of these initiatives remain behind restrictive fees, forcing many students to incur debt in order to access knowledge. The liberation of access to journal articles such as the efforts by Aaron Swartz resonate with current educational efforts offered by Massive Open Online Courses (MOOCs) that seek to make public education a right, not a privilege, such as Khan Academy. The production of a literacy ladder is associated to the production of Commons not only as pool of resources but also as social systems. As has been outlined by De Angelis, a Commons as a social system needs three constituent pillars:

- pooled material/immaterial resources or commonwealth.
- a community of commoners, that is subjects willing to share, pool, claim, commonwealth.
- commoning, or doing in common, that is a specific multifaceted social labour (activity, praxis), through which commonwealth and the community of commoners are (re)produced together with the (re)production of stuff, social relations, affects, decisions, cultures.[23]

It is his second and third points on which we should concentrate today's efforts and practices. The pursuit of competition as a form of progress has proven to be ill-equipped for allowing democratic access to knowledge production. The act of populating the literacy ladder with Open Source contributions, technical documentation or publicly available educational materials are acts of "commoning" that slowly start to identify emergent commoners who understand that a literacy ladder should operate as a form of "Commonfare,"[24] or socially produced and collectively sustained social welfare. What is obtained from this move, as has been argued by social scientist Brigitte Kratzwald, is the possibility to re-think welfare through the lens of the Commons, offering an opportunity for citizens to take control and device bottom-up rules for organization. Commoning becomes a form of "self-provision," taking responsibility for the management of shared resources.[25] Such new commons-driven organizations should not be thought to replace provisions established by the state but to complement them, generating civic organizations that can negotiate both with the state and the market.

There is a risk that an Open Source approach wherein knowledge is produced socially could be exploited and utilized as foundational knowledge for lucrative enterprises. This presents a persistent thread of market enclosure that places shared common production at a disadvantage with proprietary enterprises due to its openness and public accessibility. Efforts such as the GPL license by Richard Stallman or the Creative Commons Licenses offer fundamental tools for protection of the commonwealth. Yet more can be done to break the power asymmetry between commercial interests and their access to the Commons. This is challenging, as any initiative that would attempt to obscure or restrict access to the Commons via commercial interest runs into the risk of increasing the barrier of entry to the public. This problem gives echoes yet again of Morozov's argument, that openness is not the objective but rather a mechanism sometimes useful, sometimes problematic. Perhaps what is necessary is the development of a form of "Crypto-Commons," structures that protect themselves from enclosures, through technical, legal or organizational means. An example of this can be found in the "Climate Strike License," a software license where "developers can prohibit the use of their code by applications or companies that threaten to accelerate climate change through fossil fuel extraction."[26] As stated by the license in their website:

> Climate Strike License violates the Open Source Initiative's canonical Open Source Definition, which explicitly excludes licenses that limit re-use "in a specific field of endeavor," we feel that as tech workers, we should take responsibility in how our software is used, and that the urgency of climate change cannot be limited by the ideological position of open source software.[27]

The production of software as infrastructure for the coordination and production of Commons, as discussed in Chapter 4, does not need to subscribe to the truism of openness but needs to establish clear (and technical) commitments for lowering the barrier of entry, contributing to the production of a literacy ladder, enabling self-provision and also resisting market enclosures that operate at a market advantage. The objective of socially minded technological progress should not be technology itself but rather a community of commoners that allows for a transition between architecture dictated by the current accumulations of capital and new forms of self-provision.

From participation to self-provision

From the perspective of a hierarchy or a decision-making authority, the process of involving users or members of a community in a decision-making process is "participation." Here, participation suggests that a final decision will take into consideration some of the data collected by participatory dynamics. Architects such as Christopher Alexander[28] and lately Alejandro Aravena[29] have strongly advocated for the use of participation as a mechanism of determining the real role of the built environment in serving a community. Many of these participatory practices have become common practice, as large projects often seek for community focus groups or surveys to understand the potential risks and perception from the public. As architect Alastair Parvin explains:

> Traditionally, housing architects have aspired to work on one-off houses for wealthy clients, or large speculative developments for housebuilders. The latter requires designers to engage in "consultation" (usually with local communities), or very occasionally in enabling some process of serious "participation" by future users of the design. The problem with even the most well-meaning of these forms of engagement is that they are ultimately a condescension, a brief invitation to momentarily "participate" in a process you are ultimately not in charge of, and to do so in professional terms.[30]

A participant will always engage in a conversation that has been predefined and therefore will operate under a constrained domain. In this role, a participant is bound to validate any opposition to the ideas presented but is unable to escape the possibility space, as it is a given. Parvin has determined that the motivations behind construction vary from commercial clients that seek profit in a speculative market to members of a community that seek to occupy and generate cultural value from their dwellings. Parvin has moved away from a practice of participation that entails a form of top-down decision makers in conversation with a community to a form of "self-provision," where the labor of communities supports their own living.

We cannot discuss the production of the Commons in architecture without establishing that commoners are engaging in the self-provision of a commonwealth, or a shared form of value. Participation practices orchestrated from the perspective of a hierarchy with an interest in architectural production through capital aims to retain and increase such capital. It is only in the case of public projects that the value produced by architecture can be observed to reach public access and define a commonwealth in the city, but these only constitute a very small percentage of the cities today.

The practice of self-provision is an actualization of the Common. Self-provision is an unexpected event that is able to defy a domain and the domain's frame of expectations. Self-provision can result what the market could label as inefficient or irrational models of production; heritage, culture, religion or personal motivations all define local forms of value. We ought to generate a design framework that is able

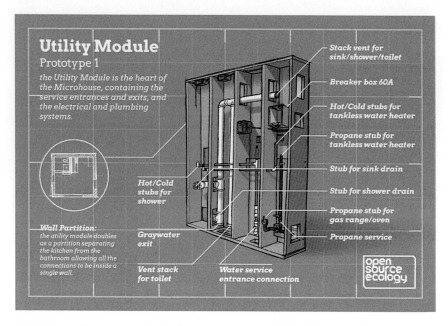

FIGURE 5.1 Open Source Ecology overview sheet of Micro-House prototype 1.

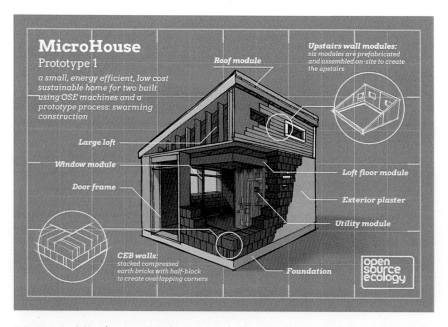

FIGURE 5.2 Microhouse 1 Development Board by Open Source Ecology. Open Source framework to contribute to the design and detailing of housing units and machines.

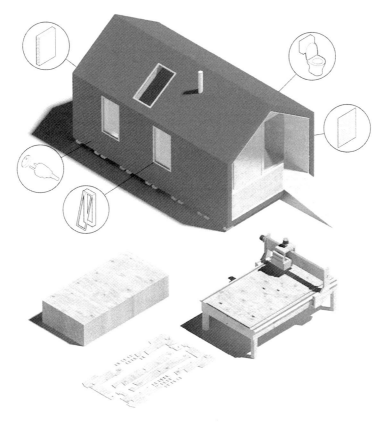

FIGURE 5.3 WikiHouse by Alastair Parvin 2012. Open Source construction set.

to incentivize and account for these forms of value, rather than consider them as externalities, or "non-professional" production.

While forms of self-provision could be linked to the "DIY" (Do-It-Yourself) movement, it is important to identify that a process of self-provision does not attempt to emphasize architecture by non-experts. On the contrary, it is architecture experts who are first called to enact the emancipatory power of self-provision contributing to the population of the literacy ladder. This is a call for a recalibration of the entrepreneurial aspirations of young architects who live the contradiction of designing concepts for houses and furniture that they could never afford, while in reality their condition of precarity doesn't allow them to afford anything beyond mass-produced furniture such as IKEA. As has been framed by the Architecture Lobby:

> Non-hierarchical work, collaboration, open-sourcing, ad hoc alliances, just-in-time delivery—these are things that architects are edging toward and that society deeply embraces. A convergence of a changing economy and a changing profession has the potential to be almost utopian. On the other

hand, entrepreneurialism and freelance labor, equally central to this new economy, might be another word for precarity, individualism, competition, and the inability to identify as a class in need of common security. In short, Entrepreneurialism might just be neoliberalism's dream child.[31]

The expertise of designers has been dissociated from the value proposition acknowledged by the market. Peer-enforced competition and a scarcity of clients sustain the "starchitect" ideal. It begs for a recalibration of objectives, allowing accumulated knowledge in the hands of highly skilled designers to reach production, connecting with immediate local environments as opposed to generating free proposals for international competitions.

There are examples where architects engage in the production of architecture as a self-commission but go beyond the simple construction of their own dwelling. The case study of the Open City (1971) located in Ritoque, north of Valparaiso in Chile, allows speculation on the critical potential of an architecture that is developed in common. For the Open City project, professors, architects, artists and designers founded the Amereida Professional Services Cooperative with the objective of combining life, work and study. The cooperative was intended to ensure the longevity of the project, as it was established as a not-for-profit foundation, the assets of which are non-transferable.[32] Documented by Rodrigo Pérez de Arce and Fernando Pérez Oyarzun, the project was founded as an autonomous initiative and had strict budgetary restrictions. The architectural production is a collective form of authorship due to its progressive and cooperative methodology. No single author has received credit for a vast collection of architectural projects developed over several decades in the Open City.

FIGURES 5.4–5.6 Hospederia de la Entrada, Cooperativa Amereida, Ciudad Abierta, Ritoque, Chile.

Source: Images courtesy of Amereida

The autonomous nature of the Open City project allowed for the project to live outside disciplinary or market influences, even though it was well known in Chile at the time. It wasn't necessarily a rejection or a countermovement to global trends but an opportunity to define a local value system, deeply rooted in a cultural practice of art in day-to-day life. As Pérez de Arce and Pérez Oyarzun present it:

> In the case of the Valparaiso School, the objective of collective work takes a greater scope and radicalism. And not only because of the weight of a

community of interests which went beyond that of the work environment, but because for the School, this collective dimension represented a value in itself; it formed part of a vision which transcended the boundaries of architecture to provide a glimpse of the possibility of an art made by all.[33]

The collective nature of the project described by Pérez de Arce and Pérez Oyarzun denotes an architecture produced for and from the Commons as a form of self-provision that advances and develops a social infrastructure for its further growth. The formal freedoms explored by the architecture of the Open City give evidence that an architecture developed with local codes does not need to adhere to the economics of austerity. Architecture by the Commons can be gratuitous and redundant, as it does not respond to any international canon or standard. Inequality and environmental awareness are emerging conflicts of our time and have been the driving force for collectives worldwide; what is needed is for architecture to define a design framework for collective action and the materialization of such emerging values.

Architecture for the Commons

Throughout this book, the potential threats to democratic and participatory societies from the perspective of design have been discussed. Trends have been identified that have augmented and accelerated the growth of economic inequality in the pursuit of technological progress. It has become imperative to question the metrics of value that deserve acknowledgement, as the continuation of a inward-looking or autopoietic tradition of disciplinary practice of architecture outlines a future with further power asymmetries.

It is no longer an option not to question and reflect on the ethos of our production. The production of value and meaning begs the identification of who is the recipient of such value and challenges us to consider forms of practice that align with progressive ideologies. This book has identified a recipient of value in the form of the Commons: not only in the disembodied collective knowledge that we share but also in the social systems of commoners that contribute to local and global knowledge scaffolds for rendering others with opportunities.

We have determined that the concentration of capital has found in vertical integration a mechanism to drive efficiency, but its implementation further exacerbates an asymmetric distribution of wealth. Discrete Architecture has been offered as an alternative, where a design framework can give rise to cooperation and coordination between different parties. Understanding parts in design establishes value for distributed systems, resisting the rise of monopolies, both economic and ideological.

This volume has put forward the idea that geometry can encapsulate knowledge and that repeatable solutions under a discrete framework can lead toward value production in the form of combinatorial surplus. The design of encapsulated knowledge into discrete tectonics is an act of commoning seeking to develop positive externalities through a process of social appropriation.

The role of parts and discrete tectonics allows designers to design down the threshold of access, enabling a dialogue between expert users that can embed knowledge and cooperative coordination into objects that share some degree of compatibility. The proposition of a discrete paradigm offers a non-unified framework for local coordination and self-provision. It does not attempt to establish totalistic guidelines but rather encourages local dialogues between autonomous units.

We have discussed how digital platforms can offer opportunities for education and self-provision but are in urgent need of redesign and regulation, as contemporary examples have become mechanisms for extractivism and behavior manipulation, able to erode democracy. Digital platforms and information sharing should seek not only openness but also clear objectives aligned with social progress. Without this, we will continue seeing Open Source projects in the hands of corporations accentuating the social struggles of our time. Knowledge propagation has been discussed not only through technical mechanisms like Open Source but also through the construction of infrastructure that could populate a literacy ladder, designing down the barrier of entry and supporting social mobility.

Platforms play an important role in the global adoption of digital networks for the generation and reproduction of culture. This comes with increasing issues and ethical imperatives as commercial enterprises have exploited underregulated digital networks for the collection of capital and market advantage. Still, the democratization of platform production has allowed for new voices to design alternative forms of interactions, considering and respecting the value of social production and effectively developing mechanisms for local value to remain in the hands of those to produce it.

Finally, the role of Commons as social systems has been identified in their capacity to populate a literacy ladder. This ladder breaks the behavioral modification and predictability established by surveillance capitalism and allows for the proliferation of new cultural production that is not predetermined by a market logic. The diversification of value systems enabled by the Commons puts forward a reexamination of canonical and disciplinary conventions that are powerful in the discipline of architecture. It also suggests that a sense of value needs to be grown from within as a form of self-provision rather than being validated by an external body. Its existence is in itself an act of legitimization.

Architecture for the Commons is in this sense an infrastructural framework that allows for design to remain as a question mark, a blank space, an undetermined space of potential without domain or predictable *actual*. Only in its production and in resonance with its coproduction is it able to define its meaning.

Notes

1 Mark Kramer and Michael Porter, 'Creating Shared Value,' *Harvard Business Review*, January–February Issue (2011).
2 Pier Vittorio Aureli, 'The Common and the Production of Architecture,' in *Common Ground: A Critical Reader: Venice Biennale of Architecture 2012* (Marsilio, 2012), pp. 147–156.
3 Aureli, 'The Common and the Production of Architecture.'

4 Nassim Nicholas Taleb, *The Black Swan: The Impact of the Highly Improbable* (Random House, 2007).
5 Alastair Parvin et al., *A Right to Build* (Self-Published, 2011).
6 Shoshana Zuboff, *The Age of Surveillance Capitalism: The Fight for a Human Future at the New Frontier of Power* (PublicAffairs, 2019).
7 David Moon, Patrick Ruffini, and David Segal, *Hacking Politics: How Geeks, Progressives, the Tea Party, Gamers, Anarchists and Suits Teamed Up to Defeat SOPA and Save the Internet* (OR Books, 2013).
8 Moon, Ruffini, and Segal, *Hacking Politics*.
9 John Schwartz, 'An Effort to Upgrade a Court Archive System to Free and Easy,' *The New York Times*, 2009 <www.nytimes.com/2009/02/13/us/13records.html>. [accessed 2 November 2018].
10 Brian Knappenberger, *The Internet's Own Boy: The Story of Aaron Swartz*, Documentary (2014).
11 Aaron Swartz, *The Boy Who Could Change the World: The Writings of Aaron Swartz* (The New Press, 2016).
12 Elie Ayache, *The Blank Swan: The End of Probability* (Wiley, 2010).
13 Aureli, 'The Common and the Production of Architecture.'
14 Carlo Ratti and Matthew Claudel, *Open Source Architecture* (Thames & Hudson, 2015).
15 Ratti and Claudel, *Open Source Architecture*.
16 Evgeny Morozov, *To Save Everything, Click Here: The Folly of Technological Solutionism* (PublicAffairs, 2013).
17 Morozov, *To Save Everything, Click Here*.
18 Morozov, *To Save Everything, Click Here*.
19 Morozov, *To Save Everything, Click Here*.
20 Zuboff, *The Age of Surveillance Capitalism*.
21 Swartz, *The Boy Who Could Change the World*.
22 Casey Reas and Ben Fry, 'Processing,' 2001 <https://processing.org/> [accessed 10 October 2015].
23 Massimo De Angelis, *Omnia Sunt Communia: On the Commons and the Transformation to Postcapitalism (In Common)* (Zed Books, 2017).
24 'Commonfare,' *P2P Foundation*, 2017 <https://wiki.p2pfoundation.net/Commonfare>. [accessed 5 October 2018].
25 Brigitte Kratzwald, 'Rethinking the Social Welfare State in Light of the Commons,' in *The Wealth of the Commons: A World Beyond Market and State* (Levellers Press, 2013).
26 'Climate Strike Software,' 2019 <https://climatestrike.software/why-now> [accessed 11 December 2019].
27 'Climate Strike Software.'
28 Christopher Alexander, *The Oregon Experiment* (Oxford University Press, 1975).
29 Alejandro Aravena and Andres Iacobelli, *Elemental: Incremental Housing and Participatory Design Manual* (Hatje Cantz, 2016).
30 Parvin et al., *A Right to Build*.
31 Peggy Deamer, Quilian Riano, and Manuel Shvartzberg, 'Identifying the Designer as Worker,' *MASS Context,* 27 (Fall 2015), 11. Debate. <https://mascontext.com/pdf/MAS_Context_Issue27_DEBATE.pdf>.
32 Rodrigo Pérez de Arce and Fernando Pérez Oyarzún, *Valparaiso Schoo /Open City Group*, ed. by Raul Rispa (Birkhauser, 2003).
33 Pérez de Arce and Pérez Oyarzún, *Valparaiso School/Open City Group*.

References

Alexander, Christopher, *The Oregon Experiment* (Oxford University Press, New York, 1975)
Aravena, Alejandro, and Andres Iacobelli, *Elemental: Incremental Housing and Participatory Design Manual* (Hatje Cantz Verlag, Ostfildern, 2016)

Aureli, Pier Vittorio, 'The Common and the Production of Architecture,' in *Common Ground: A Critical Reader: Venice Biennale of Architecture 2012* (Marsilio, Venezia, 2012), pp. 147–156

Ayache, Elie, *The Blank Swan: The End of Probability* (Wiley, Chichester, 2010)

'Climate Strike Software,' 2019 <https://climatestrike.software/why-now> [accessed 11 December 2019]

'Commonfare,' *P2P Foundation*, 2017 <https://wiki.p2pfoundation.net/Commonfare> [accessed 5 October 2018]

Deamer, Peggy, Quilian Riano, and Manuel Shvartzberg, 'Identifying the Designer as Worker,' *MASS Context*, 27 (Fall 2015), 11. Debate.

De Angelis, Massimo, *Omnia Sunt Communia: On the Commons and the Transformation to Post-capitalism (In Common)* (Zed Books, London, 2017)

Knappenberger, Brian, *The Internet's Own Boy: The Story of Aaron Swartz, Documentary* (2014)

Kramer, Mark, and Michael Porter, 'Creating Shared Value,' *Harvard Business Review*, January–February Issue (2011)

Kratzwald, Brigitte, 'Rethinking the Social Welfare State in Light of the Commons,' in *The Wealth of the Commons: A World Beyond Market and State* (Levellers Press, Amherst, 2013)

Moon, David, Patrick Ruffini, and David Segal, *Hacking Politics: How Geeks, Progressives, the Tea Party, Gamers, Anarchists and Suits Teamed Up to Defeat SOPA and Save the Internet* (OR Books, New York and London, 2013)

Morozov, Evgeny, *To Save Everything, Click Here: The Folly of Technological Solutionism* (PublicAffairs, New York, 2013)

Parvin, Alastair, David Saxby, Cristina Cerulli, and Tatjana Schneider, *A Right to Build* (Self-Published, London, 2011)

Pérez de Arce, Rodrigo, and Fernando Pérez Oyarzún, *Valparaiso School/Open City Group*, ed. by Raul Rispa (Birkhauser, Basel, 2003)

Ratti, Carlo, and Matthew Claudel, *Open Source Architecture* (Thames & Hudson, London, 2015)

Reas, Casey, and Ben Fry, 'Processing,' 2001 <https://processing.org/> [accessed 10 October 2015]

Schwartz, John, 'An Effort to Upgrade a Court Archive System to Free and Easy,' *The New York Times*, 2009 <www.nytimes.com/2009/02/13/us/13records.html> [accessed 2 November 2018]

Swartz, Aaron, *The Boy Who Could Change the World: The Writings of Aaron Swartz* (The New Press, New York, 2016)

Taleb, Nassim Nicholas, *The Black Swan: The Impact of the Highly Improbable* (Random House, New York, 2007)

Zuboff, Shoshana, *The Age of Surveillance Capitalism: The Fight for a Human Future at the New Frontier of Power* (PublicAffairs, New York, 2019)

INDEX

Note: Page numbers in *italics* indicate figures on the corresponding page.

capitalism *see* extractivism; industrial capitalism; platform capitalism; surveillance capitalism
Catmull-Clark algorithm 40
centralized networks 97
Cheung, Kenneth 76
Cities Skylines (video game) 103–104, *104*
Claudel, Matthew 115
Climate Strike License 118
CNC technology 1
Coase, Ronald 94–95
collective resistance 88
Colossal Order *104*
Combating Online Infringement and Counterfeits Act (COICA) 113
combinatorial design 78–80, 93, 94–96, 101
combinatorial surplus 74–75, 90–91
combinatorics, defined 79
Commonfare 117–118
Common Goods 22
Common'hood (video game) 105–106, *106*
Common-Pool Resources (CPRs) 21–22
Commons: as a commonwealth 112; defined 21, 23, 111; EEE as attack on 21; framing architecture's agenda 24–25; immaterial commons 23; Internet and 25–26; legacy challenge of 22–23; reconstruction of 28, 110–111; as social systems 22, 29, 117, 124; as third sphere of action 23; unorganized exploitation 21
complex adaptive systems (CAS) 62
composites 13
computation 88
computational design 47, *59*
computer numeric control (CNC) manufacturing 13
consumer-as-producer phenomenon 26
contingent model 45–46
continuous paradigm 37–38
contour crafting manufacturing *48, 49*
copyrights 20, 89–90
Creative Commons 113
creativity: exploitation of 17–18; Internet and 25
crowd(s) 80–81, 102
crowdsourcing 18, 26, 27, 99, 107
Crypto-Commons 118
Cublets 74
curvilinearity 49–50, 51
Cypherpunks 87

data collection 13, 86
data ownership 87
data provenance 98
Deamer, Peggy 27

De Angelis, Massimo 22, 117
de Graaf, Reinier 24
DeLanda, Manuel 38
Deleuzian ontology in architecture 38
democratic platforms 96–99
Demountable Architecture 94, *96*
design patterns 80–82, 94
design production, as entry barrier 112
Digital Architecture Beyond Computers (Bottazzi) 35–36
digital citizenship 97
digital discrete vs discreteness 75
digital fabrication 1, 13, 39, 57, 64–65
digital labor 96–97
digital materials 13, 64–65, *66*
digital platforms: characteristics of 87; collaborative enterprises 96; crowd engagement and 100–101; designing biased cooperation 102; as dictators 97; Open Source 8, 29, 117; patterns 88; potentiality vs actuality 112; promoting democracy 96–99; regulations 113; self-provision and 125; social activity on 99; social content production and 86; as standardization tools 7–8, 26; trending to neoliberal exploitation 86–87; *see also* platform capitalism
Discrete Architecture 9, 59–60, 75–76, 82–83, 90, 96, 124
discrete design: automation options 76, 77; compatibility and 61; described 60; distributed robotics and 76; flat ontology 72; generative systems and 62; geometrical data structures and 72; granular assemblies and 68–72; modularity vs 60; open-ended nature of 62–63
discrete model 37, 58
dissolution of parts 57
Distributed Robotic Assembly for Timber Structures 77, *78*
distributed robotics 76–77
"Do-It-Yourself" (DIY) movement 27, 89, 94, 121–122
Durbin, Richard 87

economic inequality 8, 16–17, 18, 111, 124
economics: externalities and 19–20; extractivism and 19; free-market 50; garbage spill urbanism 50; rent-seeking 19; trickle-down 14–15, 17; *see also* neoliberal economics
EEE (extractivism, externalities and enclosures) 20–21
Elemental housing project 27, *28*

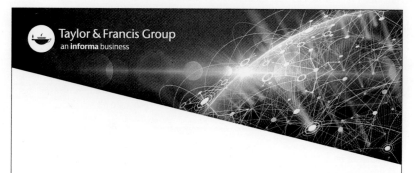